ISLAMIC COINS & THEIR VALUES

Volume 1
The Mediaeval Period

ISLAMIC COINS
& THEIR VALUES

Volume 1
The Mediaeval Period

BY
TIM WILKES

First Edition

SPINK
London
2015

Islamic Coins & Their Values
Volume 1

First published 2015
© Spink & Son Ltd.
69 Southampton Row, Bloomsbury
London, WC1B 4ET
www.spink.com

ISBN 978-1-907427-49-7

Typeset by Design to Print UK Ltd.,
9 & 10 Riverview Business Park, Forest Row, East Sussex RH18 5FS
www.designtoprintuk.com

Printed and bound in Malta
by Gutenberg Press Ltd

CONTENTS

PREFACE vi

INTRODUCTION vii

CATALOGUE

    ARAB-SASANIAN 1

    ARAB-BYZANTINE 18

    UMAYYAD 22

    ABBASID 33

    IBERIA & NORTH AFRICA 50

    EGYPT & SYRIA 74

    ARABIAN PENINSULA & EAST AFRICA 100

    AL-JAZIRA & ANATOLIA 111

    PRE-MONGOL IRAN, AFGHANISTAN & CENTRAL ASIA 142

    POST-MONGOL IRAN, AFGHANISTAN, & CENTRAL ASIA ... 195

    INDIA 234

    SOUTH-EAST ASIA 267

APPENDIX I – Islamic Mints 269

APPENDIX II – Arabic Numbers 270

APPENDIX III – Abbasid Caliphs 271

APPENDIX IV – Proper Names of Islamic Rulers 272

APPENDIX V – Image Credits 273

GENERAL INDEX 283

PREFACE

The subject of Islamic coins is one that, historically, has not been served well with reference books in the English language and even less so with regard to information on rarity and value.

The first such book was in the series of monumental volumes by Michael Mitchiner entitled *Oriental Coins & Their Values*, the first, published in 1977, covering *The World of Islam*. This work is now out of print. Nearly 20 years passed before Stephen Album published the first edition of his *Checklist of Islamic Coins* in 1993, followed by a second edition in 1998 and the most recent third edition in 2011. These works are still highly relevant for the collector but the values offered in Mitchiner's work are now dated by nearly 40 years and Album's checklist offers only a rarity guide and has no illustrations.

With the above in mind, sometime during 2012, I approached the author of this work, Tim Wilkes, with the idea of creating this book and, thankfully, he was receptive to the idea. Knowing what he knows now he may never have started the project but I am glad that he did as the result is, I hope, something that will establish itself as the standard handbook in the English language for Islamic coins for many years to come. It was created with the 'Standard Catalogue' format in mind, modelled on the highly successful *Coins of England* catalogue and the classic works by David Sear on *Greek, Roman and Byzantine Coins & Their Values*.

The original idea was to create a single-volume work covering all Islamic coinage but it soon became apparent that the work would take much longer than initially planned so it was decided to split the catalogue (at least for this first edition) into two parts, primarily in order to be able to publish the first part now so that users could get used to the format and the author can continue to work on the second part whilst receiving feedback on the first.

The task of obtaining high quality images for the catalogue was one which proved to be less painful than originally anticipated. Chris Howgego of the Ashmolean Museum, Oxford, kindly allowed us access to their vast collection of Islamic coins and we agreed with them to digitise their entire collection and they allowed us to pick and choose the images we required for this catalogue. We are extremely grateful to them for facilitating this. Many more images have been made available from the archives of various coin dealers and auctioneers and a complete list of image sources can be found in Appendix V at the end of the catalogue.

We hope you will find this book a useful and handy addition to the literature on the subject and that it will make this less-collected area of numismatics more appealing.

Philip Skingley

SPINK
London, September 2015

INTRODUCTION

The world of Islamic coins has always been a somewhat neglected area of collecting. This is a shame, because Islamic coins offer much to interest the collector, including:

- The amount of historical information found on an Islamic coin is generally far greater than that found on a contemporary European coin; since most Islamic coins do not depict images, there is more room for text. A typical Islamic coin might bear the name of the ruler, his father, his overlord, the caliph, and the mint and date of issue. Most Islamic coins, from the earliest coinages onward, are dated, whereas in Europe it did not become common practice to place the date on coins until the 16th century.
- Many Islamic coins are aesthetically pleasing due to the artistry of the calligraphy and the styles and designs used.

Many Islamic coins of the period covered by this volume were struck in far greater quantities and are far more commonly available today than contemporary European coins; consequently it is possible to build a wide-ranging representative collection even on a limited budget.

Scope of this volume

This volume covers the period from the beginning of Islamic coinage in the 1st century AH / 7th century AD up to the 10th century AH / 16th century AD. The 10th century AH marks a natural point to conclude this volume, as it saw the end of many smaller dynasties and the rise of the three great dynasties which between them would go on to rule most of the Islamic world: the Ottomans, Safavids, and Mughals. I have not imposed an arbitrary cut-off date for this volume; I have elected to list complete dynasties rather than split them between two volumes. Obviously 900 years of coinage from an area stretching from Spain to Southeast Asia is an enormous subject which cannot be covered in great detail in a single volume, so some omission and simplification was inevitable. This book is intended to serve as an introductory guide; suggestions for further reading are given at the beginning of each section.

How to use this guide

The prices given in this book are for coins in very fine (VF) condition, except for the Umayyad and Abbasid copper listings where the prices are for coins in fine (F) condition. The prices given are for coins where both the mint and date (when present) are visible; coins with illegible mints and/or dates will usually be worth less. The price given is for the most common mint and date combination within each type; rare mints and dates may be worth significantly more.

All the dates in this book are given in the Hijri (AH) calendar, signified by the letter h after the date.

Further reading

- Plant, R., *Arabic Coins and How to Read Them* (reprint due to be published in late 2015)
- Broome, M., *A Handbook of Islamic Coins*, London 1985
- Album, S., *A Checklist of Islamic Coins*, 3rd ed., Santa Rosa, 2011. This is an essential reference for any serious collector; it contains a wealth of information, both about the coins and their historical background.
- Other works are cited at the beginning of each chapter and in the dynasty listings.

Acknowledgements

Thanks are due to Philip Skingley of Spink for persuading me of the need for a book of this kind, to Stephen Lloyd of Morton & Eden Ltd for proofreading the text and for many valuable suggestions, to Matt Curtis for doing more than his fair share of running our business while I have been working on this book, and finally to my wife Lucy for all her help and support.

Tim Wilkes

CATALOGUE

ARAB-SASANIAN

For the first few decades after the Arab conquest of the Sasanian empire, the coinage of these lands consisted largely of silver drachms closely based on the design of Sasanian coins. The earliest Arab-Sasanian drachms retained the name of the Sasanian king in the obverse field in front of the king's face; this was later replaced by the name of the Arab governor (usually in Pahlavi, occasionally in Arabic). All Arab-Sasanian drachms have an Arabic inscription (most often *bism allah* – 'in the name of God') in the obverse margin. The standard reverse consists of a fire-altar and two standing attendants, to the left of which is found the date and to the right the mintname, both in Pahlavi. This coinage continued until (and beyond at a few mints) the introduction of Umayyad reform-type dirhams in 78-79h. In other Eastern areas such as Tabaristan and Central Asia the Arabs also initially continued to use the designs of the pre-conquest coinage, with minor modifications.

Walker, J., *A Catalogue of the Arab-Sasanian Coins in the British Museum*, London, 1941
Album, S., & Goodwin, T., *Sylloge of Islamic Coins in the Ashmolean, Volume 1: The Pre-Reform Coinage of the Early Islamic Period*, Oxford, 2002
Weber, E.G., *Arabo-Sasanidische Drachmen*, Bremen, 2013
Gyselen, R., *Arab-Sasanian Copper Coinage*, 2nd ed., Vienna, 2009

1

		VF
1	**Anonymous,** AR Drachm, Yazdigerd III type (common mint: SK)	$250

2

2	**Anonymous,** AR Drachm, Khusraw II type (common mints: BYŠ, SK)	$125
3	**Anonymous,** AR Drachm, Khusraw II type, mint and date in Arabic	$15,000

4

Mu'awiya, caliph (41-60h), AR Drachm (common mint: DA)

VF
$300

5

5   **'Abd Allah b. 'Amir (c.41-45h)**, AR Drachm
(common mints: BYŠ, DA)
6   - Æ Pashiz

$150

Extremely rare[1]

7

7   **Ziyad b. Abi Sufyan (45-54h)**, AR Drachm
(common mints: BYŠ, DA)

$125

8

8   **Samura b. Jundab (c.52-53h)**, AR Drachm

$400

---

[1]   Stephen Album Rare Coins, Auction 17, 19-21-September 2013, lot 89

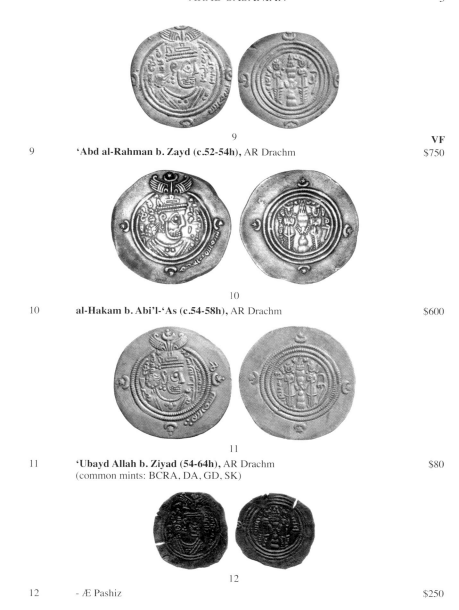

9

9   **'Abd al-Rahman b. Zayd (c.52-54h),** AR Drachm

VF
$750

10

10   **al-Hakam b. Abi'l-'As (c.54-58h),** AR Drachm

$600

11

11   **'Ubayd Allah b. Ziyad (54-64h),** AR Drachm
    (common mints: BCRA, DA, GD, SK)

$80

12

12   - Æ Pashiz

$250

13

VF

13   **'Abd Allah b. al-Zubayr (60-73h),** AR Drachm $125
      (common mints: DA, DA-GH, DA-P)

14

14   - Æ Pashiz $500

15

15   **Salm b. Ziyad (c.61-65h),** AR Drachm $100
      (common mints: HRA, MRW)

16

16   **'Abd Allah b. Khazim (fl.62-72h),** AR Drachm $150
      (common mints: BBA, MRW)
17   **al-Harith b. 'Abd Allah (64-65h),** AR Drachm $2000

18

18   **Talha b. 'Abd Allah (c.64-66h),** AR Drachm

VF
$300

19

19   **'Abd al-Malik b. Marwan, caliph (65-86h),** AR Drachm
      (common mints: DA, DA-P)

$200

20   **'Abd Allah b. 'Ariq (fl.66h),** AR Drachm   *Extremely rare*

21   **Malik b. 'Aws? (fl.66h),** AR Drachm $2000

22

22   **'Abd al-Malik b. 'Abd Allah (66-67h),** AR Drachm

$400

23

23   **'Abd al-'Aziz b. 'Abd Allah b. 'Amir (c.66-69h),** AR Drachm

$300

24

VF

24	**'Umar b. 'Ubayd Allah (67-72h),** AR Drachm (common mints: ART, BYŠ)	$80
25	**Qatan b. 'Udayy? (fl.67h),** AR Drachm	$1600
26	**Muhammad b. 'Abd Allah (fl.67h),** AR Drachm	*Extremely rare*

27

27	**Mus'ab b. al-Zubayr (c.67-71h),** AR Drachm	$400

28

28	**Qatari b. al-Fuja'a (c.69-79h),** AR Drachm	$750

29

29	**'Atiya b. al-Aswad (fl.70-77h),** AR Drachm	$275
30	**Humran b. Aban (72h),** AR Drachm	$1200

31 **'Abd al-Malik b. Abi Shaykh (fl.72h),** AR Drachm

VF
Extremely rare[2]

32
Muqatil b. Misma' (72-73h), AR Drachm
$400

32
33
Numayra b. Malik (fl.73h), AR Drachm
Extremely rare

34
Khalid b. 'Abd Allah (c.73-75h), AR Drachm
$250

34
35
Bishr b. Marwan (c.73-75h), AR Drachm, standard type
$7500

36
36 – AR Drachm, 'caliph orans' type
$7500

37
37 **'Umayya b. 'Abd Allah (c.73-77h),** AR Drachm
$600

38

38   **'Abd al-'Aziz b. 'Abd Allah (fl.74h)**, AR Drachm $400

39

39   **al-Muhallab b. Abi Sufra (c.75-79h)**, AR Drachm $125
       (common mints: ART, BYŠ, DA)
40   - Æ Pashiz $300

41

41   **al-Hajjaj b. Yusuf (75-95h)**, AR Drachm (common mint: BYŠ) $250

42

42   - AR Drachm, with radial obverse legend $1500
43   - Æ Pashiz $500

44

44	**'Abd Allah b. 'Umayya (fl.75-77h),** AR Drachm	$400
45	**al-Bara' b. Qabisa (fl.76h),** AR Drachm	*Extremely rare*
46	**al-Hakam b. Nahik (fl.77h),** AR Drachm	*Extremely rare[3]*
47	**Yazid b. al-Muhallab (78h),** AR Drachm	$1200
48	**'Abd al-Rahman b. 'Abd Allah (fl.79h),** AR Drachm	$3000
49	**al-Musayyib b. Shihr? (fl.79h),** AR Drachm	*Extremely rare*

50

50	**'Ubayd Allah b. Abi Bakra (fl.79-80h),** AR Drachm	$250
51	**'Abd Allah b. 'Amir al-Mujashi'i (fl.80h),** AR Drachm	*Extremely rare*

52

52	**'Abd al-Rahman b. Muhammad (fl.80-83h),** AR Drachm (common mint: SK)	$250
53	**'Abd Allah b. Bastam (fl.82h),** AR Drachm	*Extremely rare*

3   Morton & Eden Auction 54, 23 April 2012, lot 17

		54	**VF**
54	'Amr b. Laqit (fl.82-83h), AR Drachm		$800

55

55	Khalid b. Abi Khalid (fl.83h), AR Drachm	$3000
56	'Ubayd Allah b. 'Abd al-Rahman (c.83-84h), AR Drachm	$2500
57	'Umara b. Tamim (84-85h), AR Drachm	*Extremely rare*

58   62

58	Farroxzad, Æ Pashiz	$150
59	Yusuf b. 'Umar (119-126h), Æ Pashiz	$1000
60	Shurayk, Æ Pashiz	$400
61	Khalid b. 'Abbad, Æ Pashiz	$400
62	Daray, Æ Pashiz	$300
63	Mansur, Æ Pashiz	$400
64	Aban b. al-Walid, Æ Pashiz	$400
65	Gyanbud, Æ Pashiz	$300
66	Tegin, Æ Pashiz	$500
67	Anonymous, AR Drachm, with religious legend in place of governor's name	$5000

68

		VF
68	**Anonymous,** AR Drachm, standing caliph type	*Extremely rare*
69	**Anonymous,** AR Drachm, mihrab type	*Extremely rare*
70	**Anonymous,** Æ Pashiz, various types	$150

EASTERN SISTAN

71

71	**Anonymous,** AR Drachm	$125
72	**Sulayman (138-141h),** AR Drachm	$750
73	**Jannah,** AR Drachm	$250

74

74	**Qudama,** AR Drachm	$300

75

		VF
75	**Halil,** AR Drachm	$500
76	**Mujashi',** AR Drachm	$400
77	**Murad,** AR Drachm	$750

78

78	**Khalid,** AR Drachm	$300

79

79	**'Uthman,** AR Drachm	$300
80	**Misma',** AR Drachm	$750
81	**Ishaq,** AR Drachm	$250
82	**Bakkar,** AR Drachm	$250

83

		VF
83	**Muhammad b. Zuhayr,** AR Drachm	$600
84	**Tamim b. Sa'id (166-170h),** AR Drachm	$300
85	**'Imad,** AR Drachm	$300
86	**Rida,** AR Drachm	$250
87	**caliph al-Ma'mun (194-218h),** AR Drachm	$1500
88	**al-Layth (200-204h),** AR Drachm, countermarked type	$300

ARAB-ARMENIAN

89

89	**Anonymous,** AR Zuzun, Hormazd IV type	$15,000

90

90	**Muhammad b. Marwan,** AR Zuzun	$1200

ARAB-KHWAREZM

91	**al-Fadl b. Sulayman (166-171h),** AR Drachm	$800
92	**al-Fadl b. Sahl (196-202h),** AR Drachm	$800

ARAB-HEPHTHALITE

93

93   'Gorigo Shah', AR Drachm   **VF**
                                                                                             $1200

ARAB-BUKHARAN

94   **Khalid b. Ibrahim (137-140h),** AR Drachm   *Extremely rare*
95   **Muhammad (al-Mahdi), as heir under al-Mansur,** AR Drachm $150

96

96   **caliph al-Mahdi,** AR Drachm $125
97   **'Ali b. 'Isa (180-191h),** AR Drachm   *Extremely rare*[4]
98   **caliph al-Amin,** AR Drachm $250
99   **Dhu'l-Riyasatayn (196-202h),** AR Drachm $1200

ABBASID GOVERNORS OF TABARISTAN

Malek, H.M., *The Dabuyid Ispahbads and Early 'Abbasid Governors of Tabaristan: History and Numismatics,* London, 2004

100   **Anonymous,** AR ½-Drachm, in the name of Khurshid $125
            (posthumous)

⁴   Morton & Eden Auction 63, 22 April 2013, lot 39

101

101 **Rawh b. Hatim (146-148h),** AR ½-Drachm
102 **Muhammad (al-Mahdi), as heir under al-Mansur,** AR ½-Drachm

Extremely rare
Extremely rare[5]

103

103 **Khalid b. Barmak (149-155h),** AR ½-Drachm

$200

104

104 **'Umar b. al-'Ala (155-165h),** AR ½-Drachm

$40

105

105 **Sa'id b. Da'laj (160-163h),** AR ½-Drachm
106 **Yahya b. Mikhnaq (163-165h),** AR ½-Drachm

$40
$600

107

		VF
107	**Muqatil (164, 171-176h)**, AR ½-Drachm	$40
108	**Nusayr (168h)**, AR ½-Drachm	$2000
109	**Mihran (170h)**, AR ½-Drachm	$1500
110	**Jarir (170-172h)**, AR ½-Drachm	$150

111

111	**Sulayman (171-173h)**, AR ½-Drachm	$80

112

112	**Hani (172-176h)**, AR ½-Drachm	$40
113	**Ma'add (173h)**, AR ½-Drachm	$500
114	**'Abd Allah b. Qahtaba (174-176h)**, AR ½-Drachm	$80

115

115	**'Abd Allah b. 'Arif (176h)**, AR ½-Drachm	$250
116	**Qudayd (175h)**, AR ½-Drachm	*Extremely rare*

117

117   **Ibrahim (175-176h),** AR ½-Drachm   **VF**
$250

118

118   **'Abd Allah b. Sa'id al-Harashi (c.185-187h),** AR ½-Drachm $250
119   **al-Fadl b. Sahl (197h),** AR ½-Drachm   *Extremely rare*

120

120   **Anonymous,** AR ½-Drachm, 'AFZWT' type $30

ARAB-BYZANTINE

As was the case in the former Sasanian empire, early coinage in those parts of the Byzantine empire captured by the Arabs was based on existing prototypes. The first post-conquest coinage consisted of imitations of contemporary Byzantine copper coins. This was eventually superseded by the introduction of various different anonymous types based loosely on Byzantine designs, with legends and mintnames in either Arabic or Greek. Finally, in the 70s AH, a new uniform type was introduced depicting the standing figure of the caliph 'Abd al-Malik; copper coins of this type bear the name of the caliph, while the rare gold dinars are anonymous.

The earliest Islamic coinage of Spain and North Africa consisted of gold (and some rare copper) coins loosely based on Byzantine designs, with a variety of different types. The earliest types have modified Greek legends, while later ones have a mixture of Greek and Arabic. Many types of this series are dated with either Byzantine indiction years or AH dates. Umayyad post-reform gold and silver types were introduced much later in this region than in most of the rest of the Islamic world, in the years 97-103 AH.

Walker, J., *A Catalogue of the Arab-Byzantine and Post-Reform Umayyad Coins in the British Museum*, London, 1956
Album, S., & Goodwin, T., *Sylloge of Islamic Coins in the Ashmolean, Volume 1: The Pre-Reform Coinage of the Early Islamic Period*, Oxford, 2002
Foss, C., *Arab-Byzantine Coins*, Washington DC, 2008

121

		VF
121	**Anonymous,** AV Solidus, pseudo-Byzantine types (beware of modern forgeries of this type which are merely official Byzantine solidi with altered details)	*Extremely rare*
122	- AV Dinar, *obv.* three standing figures, *rev.* modified cross, *shahada* around	*Extremely rare*

123

123	- AV Dinar, standing caliph type, *rev.* modified cross, date around (modern forgeries of types 121-123 are frequently encountered)	*Extremely rare*
124	- Æ Fals, pseudo-Byzantine type, three standing figures	$250
125	- Æ Fals, pseudo-Byzantine type, two standing figures	$125

126

127

VF

126   - Æ Fals, pseudo-Byzantine type, standing figure $100
127   - Æ Fals, pseudo-Byzantine type, facing bust $125

128

128   - Æ Fals, two seated figures type $400
129   - Æ ½-Fals, two seated figures type $500
130   - Æ Fals, seated figure type $150

131   132

131   - Æ Fals, standing figure type (common mint: Dimashq) $125
132   - Æ Fals, two standing figures type $150

133   134

133   - Æ Fals, facing bust type (common mint: Hims) $125
134   - Æ Fals, three standing figures type $150
135   - Æ Fals, countermarked type $125

136

		VF
136	- Æ Fals, standing caliph type, *rev.* M	$250
137	- Æ 12-Nummi	$150

138

138	**'Abd al-Malik (65-86h),** Æ Fals, standing caliph type, *rev.* transformed cross (common mints: Halab, Hims)	$150

SPAIN & NORTH AFRICA

139

139	**Spain,** AV Solidus, *obv.* star, *rev.* legend across centre	$2500
140	- AV Semissis, *obv.* star, *rev.* modified cross	$8000
141	- AV Tremissis, similar	$6000

142

142	- AV Solidus, bilingual type	$15,000

143

143	**North Africa,** AV Solidus, *obv.* two facing busts, *rev.* modified cross	$12,000
144	- AV Semissis, similar	$10,000
145	- AV Tremissis, similar	$8000
146	- Æ Fals, similar	$1500
147	- Æ Fals, similar, with name of governor	$1500

148

148   - Æ Fals, *obv.* facing bust, *rev.* modified cross

VF
$1500

149

149   - AV Solidus, legend across centre on both sides $3000
150   - AV Semissis, *obv.* legend across centre, *rev.* modified cross,
               undated $3000
151   - AV Semissis, similar, with AH date   *Extremely rare*

152

152   - AV Tremissis, similar, undated $2500
153   - AV Tremissis, similar, with AH date   *Extremely rare*

154

154   - AV Solidus, bilingual type $12,000

UMAYYAD

The currency reform which took place in the years 77-78h during the reign of the caliph 'Abd al-Malik introduced standard types for gold and silver coins. Umayyad post-reform gold dinars are dated but (with a few rare exceptions – see below) do not bear the mintname; post-reform silver coins have both a mintname and a date. All post-reform gold and silver coins are anonymous. Soon after the currency reform, post-reform copper coinage gradually began to replace the existing Arab-Byzantine and Arab-Sasanian copper coins. The designs of post-reform copper fulus vary widely according to the mint of issue; many issues bear the name of a local governor or other official, and a few types have pictorial images.

During the last few years of the Umayyad caliphate (127-132h) and at the beginning of the Abbasid caliphate, silver and copper coins were issued by various commanders and officials who were in rebellion against the Umayyad caliphs. The silver dirhams are of standard type and are almost always anonymous, while the copper fulus usually bear the name of the issuer.

Walker, J., *A Catalogue of the Arab-Byzantine and Post-Reform Umayyad Coins in the British Museum*, London, 1956
Nicol, N.D., *Sylloge of Islamic Coins in the Ashmolean, Volume 2: Early Post-Reform Coinage*, Oxford, 2009

UMAYYAD GOLD

155

		VF
155	**Anonymous,** AV Dinar, no mintname, 77h	$250,000
156	- AV Dinar, no mintname, 78h	$750
157	- AV Dinar, no mintname, 79h	$600
158	- AV Dinar, no mintname, 80h	$600
159	- AV Dinar, no mintname, 81h	$600
160	- AV Dinar, no mintname, 82h	$600

161

161	- AV Dinar, no mintname, 83h	$600
162	- AV Dinar, no mintname, 84h	$600
163	- AV Dinar, no mintname, 85h	$1000
164	- AV Dinar, no mintname, 86h	$600
165	- AV Dinar, no mintname, 87h	$600
166	- AV Dinar, no mintname, 88h	$600
167	- AV Dinar, no mintname, 89h	$600
168	- AV Dinar, no mintname, 90h	$600
169	- AV Dinar, no mintname, 91h	$600

170	- AV ½-Dinar, 91h	$1200
171	- AV 1/3-Dinar, 91h	$800
172	- AV Dinar, no mintname, 92h	$600
173	- AV ½-Dinar, 92h	$1200
174	- AV 1/3-Dinar, 92h	$800
175	- AV Dinar, no mintname, 93h	$600
176	- AV Dinar, no mintname, 94h	$600
177	- AV ½-Dinar, 94h	$1500

178

178	- AV 1/3-Dinar, 94h	$800
179	- AV Dinar, no mintname, 95h	$600
180	- AV Dinar, no mintname, 96h	$600
181	- AV ½-Dinar, 96h	$1500
182	- AV 1/3-Dinar, 96h	$500
183	- AV Dinar, no mintname, 97h	$600
184	- AV 1/3-Dinar, 97h	$3000
185	- AV Dinar, no mintname, 98h	$600
186	- AV Dinar, no mintname, 99h	$600
187	- AV ½-Dinar, 99h	$3000
188	- AV 1/3-Dinar, 99h	$500

189

201

189	- AV Dinar, no mintname, 100h	$600
190	- AV ½-Dinar, 100h	$1200
191	- AV 1/3-Dinar, 100h	$400
192	- AV Dinar, no mintname, 101h	$800
193	- AV ½-Dinar, 101h	$10,000
194	- AV 1/3-Dinar, 101h	$800
195	- AV Dinar, no mintname, 102h	$800
196	- AV Dinar, no mintname, 103h	$800
197	- AV 1/3-Dinar, 103h	$1200
198	- AV Dinar, no mintname, 104h	$800
199	- AV Dinar, no mintname, 105h	$4000
200	- AV Dinar, no mintname, 106h	$600
201	- AV Dinar, no mintname, 107h	$15,000
202	- AV Dinar, no mintname, 108h	$800
203	- AV Dinar, no mintname, 109h	$800
204	- AV Dinar, no mintname, 110h	$800
205	- AV Dinar, no mintname, 111h	$600
206	- AV Dinar, no mintname, 112h	$800

		VF
207	- AV Dinar, no mintname, 113h	$800
208	- AV Dinar, no mintname, 114h	$600
209	- AV Dinar, no mintname, 115h	$800
210	- AV Dinar, no mintname, 116h	$1000
211	- AV Dinar, no mintname, 117h	$800
212	- AV Dinar, no mintname, 118h	$800
213	- AV Dinar, no mintname, 119h	$1000
214	- AV Dinar, no mintname, 120h	$800
215	- AV Dinar, no mintname, 121h	$800
216	- AV Dinar, no mintname, 122h	$800
217	- AV Dinar, no mintname, 123h	$800
218	- AV Dinar, no mintname, 124h	$800
219	- AV Dinar, no mintname, 125h	$800
220	- AV Dinar, no mintname, 126h	$800
221	- AV Dinar, no mintname, 127h	$20,000
222	- AV Dinar, no mintname, 128h	$800
223	- AV Dinar, no mintname, 129h	$1500
224	- AV Dinar, no mintname, 130h	$1500
225	- AV Dinar, no mintname, 131h	$600

226   227

226	- AV Dinar, no mintname, 132h	$12,000
227	- AV Dinar, Ifriqiya mint	$15,000

228   231

228	- AV Dinar, al-Andalus mint	$15,000
229	- AV ½-Dinar, al-Andalus mint	$15,000
230	- AV 1/3-Dinar, al-Andalus mint	$12,000
231	- AV Dinar, Ma'dan Amir al-Mu'minin mint	*Extremely rare*

232

232	- AV Dinar, Ma'dan Amir al-Mu'minin b'il-Hejaz mint	*Extremely rare*

UMAYYAD SILVER

Klat, M.G., *Catalogue of the Post-Reform Dirhams,* London, 2002

		VF
233	**Anonymous,** AR Dirham, Abarshahr mint	$250
234	- AR Dirham, Abarqubadh	$1000
235	- AR Dirham, Adharbayjan	$250
236	- AR Dirham, Ardashir Khurra	$75

237

237	- AR Dirham, Arminiya	$250

238

238	- AR Dirham, Istakhr	$75
239	- AR Dirham, Ifriqiya	$200
240	- AR Dirham, al-Andalus	$800

241

241	- AR Dirham, al-Bab	$250
242	- AR Dirham, Bizamqubadh	$1200
243	- AR Dirham, al-Basra	$75
244	- AR Dirham, Madinat Balkh al-Bayda	$1200

245

245	- AR Dirham, Balkh	$150
246	- AR Dirham, Bahurasir	$8000
247	- AR Dirham, Bihqubadh al-Asfal	$2500
248	- AR Dirham, Bihqubadh al-Awsat	$4000
249	- AR Dirham, Tawwaj	$8000
250	- AR Dirham, Shaqq al-Taymara	$400
251	- AR Dirham, al-Taymara	$75

252

252	- AR Dirham, al-Jazira	$125
253	- AR Dirham, al-Jisr	$1500
254	- AR Dirham, Jisr Shad Hurmuz	$12,000
255	- AR Dirham, Junday Sabur	$125
256	- AR Dirham, Janza	$2000
257	- AR Dirham, Jur	$1200

258

258	- AR Dirham, Jayy	$125
259	- AR Dirham, Harran	$1500
260	- AR Dirham, Hulwan	$2000
261	- AR Dirham, Dabil	$1200

262

		VF
262	- AR Dirham, Darabjird	$75
263	- AR Dirham, Dard	$5000
264	- AR Dirham, Dastawa	$150
265	- AR Dirham, Dasht Maysan	$2500

266

266	- AR Dirham, Dimashq	$40
267	- AR Dirham, Ramhurmuz	$125

268

268	- AR Dirham, al-Rayy	$200
269	- AR Dirham, Sabur	$50
270	- AR Dirham, al-Samiya	$75
271	- AR Dirham, Sijistan	$250
272	- AR Dirham, Sarakhs	$400
273	- AR Dirham, Surraq	$200
274	- AR Dirham, al-Sus	$300

275

275	- AR Dirham, Suq al-Ahwaz	$100

		VF
276	- AR Dirham, Tabaristan	$1200
277	- AR Dirham, al-Furat	$300
278	- AR Dirham, Fasa	$2000
279	- AR Dirham, Fil	$3000

280

280	- AR Dirham, Qumis	$600

281

281	- AR Dirham, Kirman	$75
282	- AR Dirham, al-Kufa	$100
283	- AR Dirham, Mah	$600
284	- AR Dirham, Mah al-Basra	$600
285	- AR Dirham, Mah al-Kufa	$5000
286	- AR Dirham, Mahay	$125
287	- AR Dirham, al-Mubaraka	$150
288	- AR Dirham, Marw	$75
289	- AR Dirham, Mazinan	$8000
290	- AR Dirham, Manadhir	$100
291	- AR Dirham, Mihrjanqudhaq	$6000
292	- AR Dirham, Maysan	$400
293	- AR Dirham, Nahr Tira	$125
294	- AR Dirham, al-Niq	$8000
295	- AR Dirham, Herat	$125
296	- AR Dirham, Hamadan	$200

297

297	- AR Dirham, Wasit	$25
298	- AR Dirham, contemporary North African imitation of Wasit, star above reverse legend	$250

299

| 299 | - AR Dirham, no mintname | VF *Extremely rare* |

(other mints are known, all extremely rare)

UMAYYAD POST-REFORM COPPER

		F
300	**al-Walid I (86-96h),** Æ Fals	$150
301	**Anonymous,** Æ Fals, al-Urdunn	$100
302	- Æ Fals, Arminiya	$250
303	- Æ Fals, al-Iskandariya	$250
304	- Æ Fals, Isbahan	$250
305	- Æ Fals, Istakhr	$125
306	- Æ Fals, Anbulus	$400
307	- Æ Fals, al-Andalus	$100
308	- Æ Fals, Iliya	$150
309	- Æ Fals, al-Bab	$250
310	- Pb Fals, al-Bahrayn	$400
311	- Æ Fals, Barda'a	$600
312	- Æ Fals, al-Basra	$150
313	- Æ Fals, Busra	$150

314

314	- Æ Fals, Ba'albak	$20
315	- Æ Fals, Balikh	$40
316	- Æ Fals, Bayt Jabrin	$200
317	- Æ Fals, Baysan	$150
318	- Æ Fals, Tanukh	$75
319	- Æ Fals, Jibrin	$150
320	- Æ Fals, Jurjan	$100
321	- Pb Fals, Jurjan	$250
322	- Æ Fals, Jerash	$300
323	- Æ Fals, Jayy	$250
324	- Æ Fals, Harran	$40
325	- Æ Fals, Halab	$25

F

326	- Æ Fals, Hims	$25
327	- Æ Fals, Dabil	$500
328	- Æ Fals, Dar'at	$150

329   337

329	- Æ Fals, Dimashq	$25
330	- Æ Fals, al-Ramla	$60
331	- Æ Fals, al-Ruha	$125
332	- Æ Fals, al-Rayy	$250
333	- Æ Fals, Zaranj	$200
334	- Æ Fals, Sabur	$150
335	- Æ Fals, Sarmin	$100
336	- Æ Fals, Saffuriya	$400
337	- Æ Fals, Tabariya	$80
338	- Æ Fals, Tanja	$600
339	- Æ Fals, 'Asqalan	$300
340	- Æ Fals, 'Akka	$150
341	- Æ Fals, 'Amman	$75
342	- Æ Fals, Ghazza	$500

343   345

343	- Æ Fals, al-Fustat	$125
344	- Æ Fals, Filastin	$125
345	- Æ Fals, Qinnasrin	$20
346	- Æ Fals, al-Kufa	$275
347	- Æ Fals, Ludd	$150
348	- Æ Fals, Ma'arat Misrin	$150
349	- Æ Fals, al-Madina Ma'dan Amir al-Mu'minin	$1500
350	- Æ Fals, Misr	$80
351	- Æ Fals, Manbij	$150
352	- Æ Fals, al-Mawsil	$60
353	- Æ Fals, Nasibin	$300
354	- Æ Fals, Wasit	$80
355	- Æ Fals, Yubna	$500

356

		F
356	- Æ Fals, no mint	$15
357	- Pb Fals, no mint	$150

(other mints are known, all extremely rare)

REVOLUTIONARY PERIOD

Wurtzel, C., 'The Coinage of the Revolutionaries in the Late Umayyad Period', *ANS Museum Notes 23*, New York, 1978

		VF
358	**Anonymous,** AR Dirham, Istakhr mint	$1500
359	- AR Dirham, Balkh	$3000
360	- AR Dirham, Tanbarak	$15,000
361	- AR Dirham, al-Taymara	$800

362

362	- AR Dirham, Jayy	$500
363	- AR Dirham, Darabjird	$6000
364	- AR Dirham, Ramhurmuz	$1000
365	- AR Dirham, al-Rayy	$1500

366

366	- AR Dirham, Gharshistan	*Extremely rare*

367

367   - AR Dirham, al-Kufa $400
368   - AR Dirham, Mahay $800

369

369   - AR Dirham, Marw $500

                                   F
370   **Abu Muslim,** Æ Fals $150

371

371   **al-Dahhak b. Qays (fl.128-130h),** Æ Fals $250
372   **Imran b. Isma'il (fl.136h),** Æ Fals $300
373   **Sulayman b. 'Abd Allah, governor of Sijistan (138-140h),** $300
       Æ Fals

ABBASID

The earliest Abbasid coinage was similar to Umayyad coinage in that there were standard anonymous types for gold and silver coins. However, over the course of the first Abbasid period (132-218h) the variety of the coinage increased. From the reign of al-Mahdi (158-169h) onwards, the caliph's name normally appeared on silver dirhams, and it gradually became more common for the names of provincial governors or other officials to appear on both gold and silver coins. Starting with the reign of al-Mu'tasim (218-227h) the Abbasid coinage became much more standardized: all gold and silver coins bore the name of the caliph and no other names appeared except those of the caliphal heir and (occasionally) the caliphal vizier. The types of Abbasid copper fulus vary greatly according to the mint of issue; most Abbasid copper coins do not bear the name of the caliph. The Abbasid caliphate was conquered by the Buwayhids in 334h; for the next two hundred years the caliphs were under the control of whichever dynasty controlled their capital of Madinat al-Salam (Baghdad) and exercised little temporal power, but the name of the caliph was retained on the majority of Islamic coins struck during this period. Only in the last hundred years of the caliphate were the caliphs able to regain real power and resume regular coinage, before their final overthrow by the Mongols in 656h.

Bernardi, G., *Arabic Gold Coins Corpus I*, Trieste, 2010
Tiesenhausen, V., *Monnaies des Khalifes Orientaux*, St Petersburg, 1873 (available to view online)
Shams Eshragh, A., *Silver Coinage of the Caliphs*, London, 2010
Nicol, N.D., *Sylloge of Islamic Coins in the Ashmolean, Volume 3: Early 'Abbasid Precious Metal Coinage (to 218 AH)*, Oxford, 2012
Nicol, N.D., *Sylloge of Islamic Coins in the Ashmolean, Volume 4: Later 'Abbasid Precious Metal Coinage (from 219 AH)*, Oxford, 2012
Shamma, S., *A Catalogue of 'Abbasid Copper Coins*, London, 1998

374

			VF
374	**al-Saffah (132-136h),** AV Dinar, no mint		$400

375

375	- AR Dirham, (common mints: al-Basra, al-Kufa)	$40

376

376   **al-Mansur (136-158h),** AV Dinar, no mint $250

377

377   - AR Dirham, $40
(common mints: al-Basra, al-Rayy, al-Kufa, al-Muhammadiya,
Madinat al-Salam)

378

378   **al-Mahdi (158-169h),** AV Dinar, no mint $250

379

379   - AR Dirham, $40
(common mints: Jayy, al-Muhammadiya, Madinat al-Salam)

380   **al-Hadi (169-170h),** AV Dinar, no mint $300

381

381   - AR Dirham $125

382

382   **al-Rashid (170-193h),** AV Dinar, no mint $300
383   - AV Dinar, no mint, caliph's name in reverse field $8000

384

384   - AR Dirham
     (common mints: Balkh, Zaranj, Ma'dan al-Shash, al-Muhammadiya, $40
     Madinat al-Salam)
385   **Zubayda, wife of al-Rashid,** AR Dirham   *Extremely rare*

386

386   **al-Amin (193-198h),** AV Dinar $300

387

387   - AR Dirham (common mint: Madinat al-Salam) $40
388   - AR Dirham, with the name of the heir al-Natiq Musa   *Extremely rare*

389

389   **al-Ma'mun (194-218h),** AV Dinar $300

390

390   - AR Dirham
(common mints: Isbahan, Samarqand, al-Muhammadiya,
Madinat al-Salam)

391

391   - AR Dirham, with the name of the heir al-Rida $600
392   - AR ½-Dirham $800
393   - AR ¼-Dirham $1200

394

394   **Abu'l-Saraya al-Shaybani, rebel (199h),** AR Dirham $1200
395   *temp.* **Ibrahim (202-203h),** AV Dinar   *Extremely rare*[1]
396   - AR Dirham $600

397

397   **al-Mu'tasim (218-227h),** AV Dinar (common mint: Misr) $500

---

1   Stephen Album Rare Coins, Auction 16, 17-18 May 2013, lot 159

398

VF

398   - AR Dirham (common mint: Madinat al-Salam) $125

399

399   **al-Wathiq (227-232h),** AV Dinar (common mint: Misr) $500

400

400   - AR Dirham (common mint: Madinat al-Salam) $150

401

401   **al-Mutawakkil (232-247h),** AV Dinar (common mint: Misr) $400
402   - AV Dinar, donative type with broad outer margin $8000
403   - AV Dinar, donative type struck on small thick flan $1200

404

404   - AR Dirham (common mints: Surra man Ra'a, Madinat al-Salam) $150

405   VF
	405	
405	- AR Dirham, donative type with broad outer margin	$1200
406	- AR Dirham, donative type struck on small thick flan	$500
407	- AR ½-Dirham, donative type	Extremely rare
408	**al-Muntasir (247-248h),** AV Dinar	$15,000

409   410
409	- AR Dirham	$800
410	**al-Musta'in (248-251h),** AV Dinar	$500
	(common mints: Samarqand, al-Shash, Misr)	

411
411	- AR Dirham	$150

412   413
412	**al-Mu'tazz (251-255h),** AV Dinar	$500
	(common mints: Surra man Ra'a, al-Shash, Misr)	
413	- AR Dirham	$150
	(common mints: Isbahan, Surra man Ra'a, Samarqand, Fars)	
414	**al-Muhtadi (255-256h),** AV Dinar	$3000
415	- AR Dirham	$400

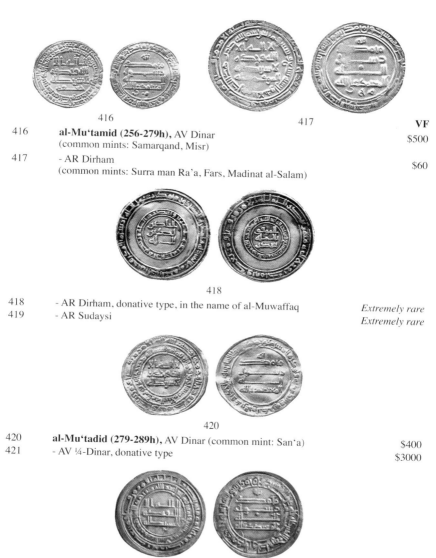

416

417

VF

416   **al-Mu'tamid (256-279h),** AV Dinar $500
        (common mints: Samarqand, Misr)

417   - AR Dirham $60
        (common mints: Surra man Ra'a, Fars, Madinat al-Salam)

418

418   - AR Dirham, donative type, in the name of al-Muwaffaq   *Extremely rare*
419   - AR Sudaysi   *Extremely rare*

420

420   **al-Mu'tadid (279-289h),** AV Dinar (common mint: San'a) $400
421   - AV ¼-Dinar, donative type $3000

422

422   - AR Dirham $40
        (common mints: Surra man Ra'a, Madinat al-Salam, Wasit)

423

		VF
423	- AR Dirham, donative type	$1500
424	- AR ½-Dirham, donative type	$1200

425 426

425	**al-Muktafi (289-295h)**, AV Dinar (common mint: Misr)	$400
426	- AR Dirham	$40
	(common mints: Surra man Ra'a, Madinat al-Salam, Wasit)	

427

427	**al-Muqtadir (295-320h)**, AV Dinar	$300
	(common mints: al-Ahwaz, Tustar min al-Ahwaz, Suq al-Ahwaz, Madinat al-Salam, Misr)	

428 429

428	- AV Dinar, donative type with broad outer margin	$8000
429	- AV Amiri Dinar	$300
430	- AV ¼-Dinar, donative type	$4000

431

431   - AR Dirham
     (common mints: Surra man Ra'a, Madinat al-Salam, Wasit)

VF

$40

432

432   - AR Dirham, donative type with broad outer margin

$1000

433

433   - AR Dirham, donative type, no mintname, dated
434   - AR Dirham, donative type, ornamental designs

$4000
$4000

435

435   - AR Dirham, donative type, hare on both sides

$8000

436

436   - AR Dirham, donative type, bull and horseman

Extremely rare

437

437   **al-Qahir (320-322h),** AV Dinar (common mint: al-Ahwaz) $300

438   439

438   - AV Dinar, donative type with broad outer margin   *Extremely rare*
439   - AV Amiri Dinar $600

440

440   - AR Dirham (common mint: Madinat al-Salam) $40

441

441   **al-Radi (322-329h),** AV Dinar $300
    (common mints: al-Ahwaz, Tustar min al-Ahwaz, Suq al-Ahwaz,
    Misr)

442

442   - AV Dinar, donative type, no mintname, dated $12,000

443

443   - AV Amiri Dinar

VF
$400

444

444   - AR Dirham
    (common mints: Surra man Ra'a, Madinat al-Salam, Wasit) $40

445   - AR Dirham, donative type with broad outer margin

$1500

446   449

446   - AR Dirham, donative type, no mintname, dated $1200
447   - AR 1/3-Dirham, donative type $3000
448   - AR Sudaysi $150
449   **al-Muttaqi (329-333h),** AV Dinar $400
    (common mint: Madinat al-Salam)

450

450   - AV Dinar, donative type with broad outer margin   *Extremely rare*

451

VF

451 - AV Amiri Dinar $1000

452

452 - AR Dirham (common mints: al-Basra, Madinat al-Salam) $40

453

453 - AR Dirham, donative type *Extremely rare*
454 - AR Sudaysi *Extremely rare*

455

455 **al-Mustakfi (333-334h),** AV Dinar $3000

456

456 - AV Amiri Dinar $500

457

457	- AR Dirham (common mint: Madinat al-Salam)	$200
458	**al-Muti' (334-363h),** AV Dinar (Arabian mints only)	$2500

459

459	- AV Amiri Dinar	$800

460

462

460	- AR Dirham, donative type, bull and horseman	*Extremely rare*
461	- AR Dirham, donative type, legends only	*Extremely rare*
462	- AR Sudaysi	$50

463

463	**al-Muqtadi (467-487h),** AV Dinar	$3000
464	**al-Mustazhir (487-512h),** AV Dinar	$2500
465	**al-Mustarshid (512-529h),** AV Dinar	*Extremely rare*
466	**al-Muqtafi (530-555h),** AV Dinar	$2500
467	**al-Mustanjid (555-566h),** AV Dinar	$1200
468	**al-Mustadi (566-575h),** AV Dinar	$1000

469

VF
$400

469 **al-Nasir (575-622h)**, AV Dinar
(common mint: Madinat al-Salam)

470

$1000

470 **al-Zahir (622-623h)**, AV Dinar

471 472

471 **al-Mustansir (623-640h)**, AV Dinar
(common mint: Madinat al-Salam)
472 - AR Dirham (common mint: Madinat al-Salam)
473 - AR ½-Dirham

$600

$250
$150

474

474 **al-Musta'sim (640-656h)**, AV Dinar

$500

475

| 475 | - AR Dirham (common mint: Madinat al-Salam) | $250 |

476　　　　　　　　　　477

476	- AR ½-Dirham	$150
477	- AR 1/3-Dirham	$750
478	- AR ¼-Dirham	$500

ABBASID COPPER

		F
479	Æ Fals, Arran mint	$200
480	Æ Fals, Arrajan	$250
481	Æ Fals, Ardashir Khurra	$50
482	Æ Fals, Arminiya	$300
483	Æ Fals, Istakhr	$30
484	Æ Fals, Ifriqiya	$200
485	Æ Fals, Amul	$500
486	Æ Fals, Bukhara	$60
487	Æ Fals, Barda'a	$250
488	Æ Fals, al-Basra	$150

489

489	Æ Fals, Balad	$100
490	Æ Fals, Balkh	$75
491	Æ Fals, Tawwaj	$250
492	Æ Fals, Jabal al-Fidda	$500
493	Æ Fals, Jubayl	$400
494	Æ Fals, Jurjan	$60

495   500   **F**

		F
495	Æ Fals, al-Jazira	$30
496	Æ Fals, Jiruft	$200
497	Æ Fals, Halab	$75
498	Æ Fals, Hims	$60
499	Æ Fals, Dabil	$400
500	Æ Fals, Dimashq	$80
501	Æ Fals, Ra's al-'Ayn	$150
502	Æ Fals, al-Rafiqa	$40
503	Æ Fals, al-Raqqa	$150
504	Æ Fals, Ramhurmuz	$300
505	Æ Fals, al-Ramla	$150
506	Æ Fals, al-Rayy	$150
507	Æ Fals, Zaranj	$150
508	Æ Fals, Sabur	$50
509	Æ Fals, Sijistan	$150
510	Æ Fals, Samarqand	$100
511	Æ Fals, Sinjar	$250
512	Æ Fals, Suq al-Ahwaz	$150
513	Æ Fals, al-Shash	$60
514	Æ Fals, Shiraz	$125
515	Æ Fals, Sur	$150
516	Æ Fals, Tabaristan	$200
517	Æ Fals, Trablus	$200
518	Æ Fals, Tarsus (cast)	$80
519	Æ Fals, al-'Abbasiya	$200
520	Æ Fals, 'Irqa	$150
521	Æ Fals, 'Akka	$150
522	Æ Fals, Ghazza	$200
523	Æ Fals, Fars	$200
524	Æ Fals, Fasa	$100
525	Æ Fals, al-Quds	$300

526

526	Æ Fals, Qinnasrin	$125
527	Æ Fals, Qaysariya	$500
528	Æ Fals, Kafr Tutha	$200
529	Æ Fals, Kurat al-Mahdiya min Fars	$80

		F
530	Æ Fals, al-Kufa	$25
531	Æ Fals, Ludd	$300
532	Æ Fals, Mah al-Kufa	$300

533

| 533 | Æ Fals, al-Muhammadiya | $125 |

534

534	Æ Fals, Madinat al-Salam	$40
535	Æ Fals, Marw	$150
536	Æ Fals, Misr	$80
537	Æ Fals, al-Masisa	$75
538	Æ Fals, al-Mawsil	$50
539	Æ Fals, Nasibin	$80
540	Æ Fals, Nishapur	$250
541	Æ Fals, Nihavand	$300
542	Æ Fals, Herat	$150
543	Æ Fals, Hamadan	$150
544	Æ Fals, Wasit	$150
545	Æ Fals, no mint	$50

(other mints are known, all extremely rare)

IBERIA & NORTH AFRICA

In 138h 'Abd al-Rahman, an Umayyad prince who had managed to escape from Damascus after the Abbasid revolution in 132h, arrived in Spain and founded the emirate (later caliphate) which would last for nearly three centuries. After the collapse of the caliphate in the early 5th century AH, Spain was divided into various local principalities. Abbasid control did extend briefly into part of the Maghreb (modern Morocco, Algeria, and Tunisia), but local dynasties, initially the Idrisids and Aghlabids, soon began to assert their independence. In the late 5th century AH the Almoravids succeeded in gaining control over the Maghreb and most of Muslim Spain, but their rule did not last long; after their fall power once again devolved to various local rulers. Most of Spain was soon reconquered by the Christian kingdoms, leaving only the Nasrid kingdom in the far south, which would endure until 897h. In the Maghreb the Almoravids were succeeded by the Almohads, who were in turn succeeded by the Hafsids, Ziyanids and Merinids. The 10th century AH saw the conquest of the eastern part of the Maghreb by the Ottomans and the establishment of the Sa'dian kingdom of Morocco.

Miles, G.C., *Coins of the Spanish Muluk al-Tawa'if*, New York, 1954
Vives y Escudero, A., *Monedas de las Dinastias Arabigo-Españolas*, Madrid, 1893
Hazard, H.W., *The Numismatic History of Late Medieval North Africa*, ANS Numismatic Studies No. 8, New York, 1952

UMAYYAD OF SPAIN

Miles, G.C., *The Coinage of the Umayyads of Spain*, 2 vols., New York, 1950

546

		VF
546	*temp*. **'Abd al-Rahman I (138-172h)**, AR Dirham	$125

547

547	*temp*. **Hisham I (172-180h)**, AR Dirham	$150

548

VF

| 548 | *temp.* **al-Hakam I (180-206h),** AR Dirham | $100 |

549

| 549 | *temp.* **'Abd al-Rahman II (206-238h),** AR Dirham | $100 |

550

550	*temp.* **Muhammad I (238-273h),** AR Dirham	$100
551	- Æ Fals	$250
552	**al-Mundhir (273-275h),** AR Dirham	*Extremely rare*
553	**'Abd Allah (275-300h),** AR Dirham	*Extremely rare*

554

| 554 | **'Abd al-Rahman III (300-350h),** AV Dinar | $2500 |
| 555 | - AV ¼-Dinar | $800 |

556

VF

| 556 | - AR Dirham | $60 |

557

| 557 | **al-Hakam II (350-366h)**, AV Dinar | $1500 |

558

| 558 | - AR Dirham | $50 |
| 559 | **Hisham II, 1st reign (366-399h)**, AV Dinar | $1500 |

560   562

560	- AR Dirham	$50
561	**Muhammad II (399-400h)**, AV Dinar	$2500
562	- AR Dirham	$150

563

| 563 | **Sulayman, 1st reign (400h)**, AV Dinar | $2500 |

564

565

| 564 | - AR Dirham | **VF** |
| | | $150 |

| 565 | **Hisham II, 2nd reign (400-403h),** AV Dinar | $2000 |

566

| 566 | - AR Dirham | $125 |

567

567	**Sulayman, 2nd reign (403-407h),** AV Dinar	$4000
568	- AR Dirham	$250
569	**'Abd al-Rahman V (414h),** AR Dirham	*Extremely rare*
570	**Muhammad III (414-416h),** AV Dinar	*Extremely rare*
571	**Hisham III (418-422h),** AV Dinar	*Extremely rare*
572	- AV fractional Dinar	*Extremely rare*
573	**Anonymous, Æ Fals,** undated	$250

HAMMUDID OF MALAGA

574   **al-Nasir 'Ali (400-408h)**, AV Dinar

575

| 575 | - AR Dirham | $300 |
| 576 | **al-Ma'mun al-Qasim (408-414h)**, AV Dinar | $5000 |

577

577   - AR Dirham $250

578

578   **al-Mu'tali Yahya (412-427h)**, AV Dinar $5000

579

| 579 | - AR Dirham | $250 |
| 580 | **al-'Ali Idris II (434-446h)**, AR Dirham | $300 |

581

581   **al-Mahdi Muhammad I (438-446h)**, BI Dirham $200

HAMMUDID OF WADI LAU

582

		VF
582	**Hasan (fl.441h)**, BI Dirham	$400

'ABBADID

583	**al-Mu'tadid 'Abbad (433-461h)**, AV Dinar	$1500
584	- AV fractional Dinar	$400

585

585	- AR Dirham	$300

586

586	**al-Mu'tamid Muhammad (461-484h)**, AV Dinar	$2500
587	- AV fractional Dinar	$500
588	- AR Dirham	$500

ZIRID OF GRANADA

589	*temp.* **Badis b. Habbus (c.429-465h)**, AV fractional Dinar	$300
590	- AR Dirham	$300
591	**al-Mu'izz Tamim b. Buluggin (459-483h)**, AV Dinar	*Extremely rare*

'AMIRID OF VALENCIA

592	**'Abd al-'Aziz al-Mansur (412-452h)**, AV fractional Dinar	$150
593	- AR Dirham	$300
594	**'Abd al-Malik al-Muzaffar (452-457h)**, AR Dirham	$400

KINGS OF MALLORCA

595

		VF
595	**'Abd Allah al-Murtada (468-486h)**, AR Dirham	$1200
596	**Nasir al-dawla Mubashir (486-508h)**, BI Dirham	$750

SLAVE KINGDOM OF DENIA

597	**Mujahid (c.404-436h)**, AV fractional Dinar	$1500

598

598	- AR Dirham	$600

599

599	**Iqbal al-dawla 'Ali (436-468h)**, AR Dirham	$400

HUDID OF DENIA

600	**'Imad al-dawla Mundhir (474-483h)**, BI Dirham	$400
601	**Sayyid al-dawla Sulayman (483-492h)**, BI Dirham	$400

HUDID OF ZARAGOZA

602	**Taj al-dawla Sulayman (438-441h)**, AV fractional Dinar	$500
603	- AR Dirham	$800

604

		VF
604	'Imad al-dawla Ahmad I (441-475h), BI Dirham	$300
605	al-Musta'in Ahmad II (476-503h), BI Dirham	$300

HUDID OF TUDELA

606	al-Zafir Mundhir (fl.438-442h), BI Dirham	$1200

KINGDOM OF TORTOSA

607

607	Muqatil (c.427-445h), AR Dirham	$750

DHU'L-NUNID OF TOLEDO

608	al-Zafir Isma'il (c.423-435h), AV fractional Dinar	$400
609	Sharaf al-dawla Yahya I (435-467h), AV fractional Dinar	$400

610

610	- AR Dirham	$800

SUMAYDIHID OF ALMERIA

611	Anonymous, AR Dirham	$150
612	al-Mu'tasim Muhammad (443-484h), AR Dirham	$500

AFTASID OF BADAJOZ

VF

| 613 | **al-Mutawakkil 'Umar (460-487h),** AR Dirham | $400 |
| 614 | - AR fractional Dirham | $125 |

TAIFAS ALMORAVIDES

| 615 | **Anonymous,** AV Dinar | $2500 |

KINGS OF CORDOBA

| 616 | **Hamdin b. Muhammad (c.539-540h),** AV Dinar | $4000 |

617   618

617	- AR Qirat	$150
618	**Ibn Wazir (c.540-542h),** AR Qirat	$250
619	**Anonymous,** AV Dinar, in the name of the Banu Tashfin	$6000

KINGS OF MURCIA

620   621

620	**Muhammad b. Sa'd (542-567h),** AV Dinar	$2500
621	- BI Dirham	$1000
622	- BI fractional Dirham	$150

KINGS OF MERTOLA & SILVES

623

| 623 | **Ahmad b. Qasi (fl.539-546h),** AR Qirat | $1200 |
| 624 | **Sidray b. Wazir (546-552h),** AR Qirat | $1200 |

HUDID OF MURCIA

		VF
625	**Muhammad b. Yusuf (621-635h),** AR Dirham	$300
626	*temp.* **Baha' al-dawla (c.639-659h),** AV ½-Dinar	$1500
627	- AV ¼-Dinar	$1000

AMIRS OF LORCA

628	*temp.* **Ibn Asli (638-642h),** BI square Dirham	$1000

ALGARVE

629

629	**Musa b. Muhammad (631-660h),** AR square Dirham	$400

NASRID

630

630	**Muhammad I (630-672h),** AR square Dirham	$750
631	**Muhammad IV (724-734h),** AV Dinar	$3000
632	**Yusuf I b. Isma'il (734-755h),** AV Dinar	$2500
633	**Muhammad V (755-761h),** AV Dinar	$3000

634

634	- AR square 2-Dirhams	$1000
635	**Muhammad VIII (819-821, 831-832h),** AV Dinar	$4000

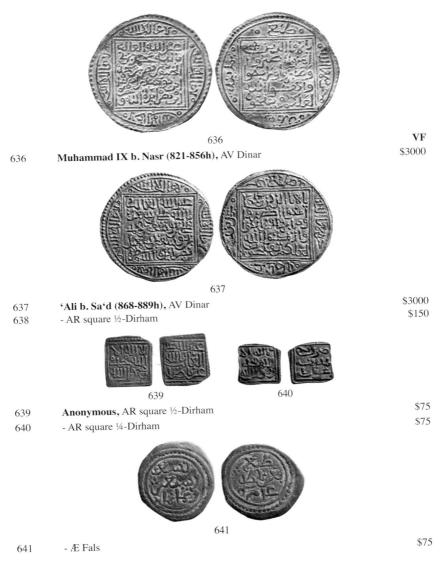

636

VF
$3000

636   **Muhammad IX b. Nasr (821-856h)**, AV Dinar

637

637   **'Ali b. Sa'd (868-889h)**, AV Dinar $3000
638   - AR square ½-Dirham $150

639   640

639   **Anonymous,** AR square ½-Dirham $75
640   - AR square ¼-Dirham $75

641

641   - Æ Fals $75

IDRISID

Eustache, D., *Corpus des Dirhams Idrisites et Contemporains*, Rabat, 1970-1971

		VF
	642	
642	**Idris I (172-175h),** AR Dirham	$150
	643	
643	**Idris II (175-213h),** AR Dirham	$125
644	- Æ Fals	$500
	645	
645	**Muhammad b. Idris (213-221h),** AR Dirham	$150
646	**Yahya b. Idris (c.213-233h),** AR Dirham	$300
	647	
647	**'Ali b. Muhammad (221-234h),** AR Dirham	$300
648	**'Isa b. Idris (225-233h),** AR Dirham	$300
	649	
649	**Yahya I b. Muhammad (234-249h),** AR Dirham	$300

KHARIJITES

650

VF

650   **Khalaf b. al-Muda' (fl.175-176h),** AR Dirham $125

651

651   **Anonymous,** AR Dirham $300

IDRISID CONTEMPORARIES

652   **Ibrahim (fl.177-179h),** AR Dirham $500

653

653   **Ma'zuz b. Talut (fl.223-224h),** AR Dirham $500

AGHLABID

al-'Ush, M.A., *Monnaies Aglabides,* Damascus, 1982

654

654   **Ibrahim I (184-196h),** AV Dinar (anonymous) $5000

655

		VF
655	- AR Dirham	$250
656	- Æ Fals	$100
657	**'Abd Allah I (196-201h)**, AV Dinar	$400

658

658	- AR Dirham	$250
659	**Ziyadat Allah I (201-223h)**, AV Dinar	$400
660	- AV ¼-Dinar	$600

661

661	- AR Dirham	$200

662   665

662	**al-Aghlab (223-226h)**, AV Dinar	$500
663	- Æ Fals	$150
664	**Muhammad I (226-242h)**, AV Dinar	$400
665	**Ahmad (242-249h)**, AV Dinar	$400
666	**Ziyadat Allah II (249-250h)**, AV Dinar	$5000

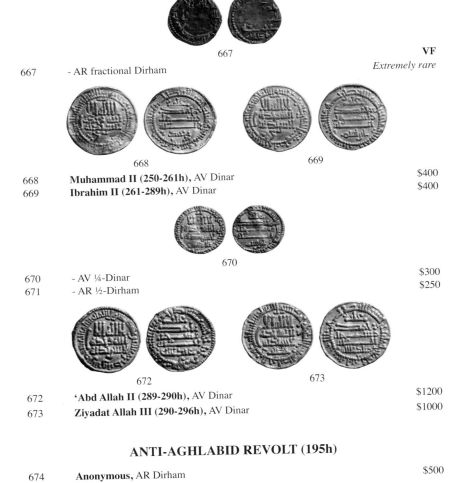

667

VF
Extremely rare

667   - AR fractional Dirham

668   669

668   **Muhammad II (250-261h)**, AV Dinar $400
669   **Ibrahim II (261-289h)**, AV Dinar $400

670

670   - AV ¼-Dinar $300
671   - AR ½-Dirham $250

672   673

672   **'Abd Allah II (289-290h)**, AV Dinar $1200
673   **Ziyadat Allah III (290-296h)**, AV Dinar $1000

ANTI-AGHLABID REVOLT (195h)

674   **Anonymous**, AR Dirham $500

SULAYMANID

675

675   **Ibrahim b. Muhammad (fl.256-258h)**, AR Dirham $1500

676

676   'Isa b. Ibrahim (fl.270-280h), AR Dirham $1200
677   Sulayman b. Muhammad (fl.276h), AR Dirham   *Extremely rare*[1]

MIDRARID

678   Muhammad b. al-Fath (321-347h), AV Dinar $600

KHAZRUNID

679   Wanudin (d. c.440h), AV Dinar $700
680   Mas'ud b. Wanudin (c.440-445h), AV Dinar $1000

ZIRID

681

681   *temp.* al-Mu'izz b. Badis (406-454h), AV Dinar $300
682   - AV ¼-Dinar $300
683   - AR fractional Dirham $100

BANU HILAL

684   Anonymous, AV Dinar $2000

BARGHAWATID OF SFAX

685

685   *temp.* **Hammu b. Malil (451-493h)**, AV Dinar

VF
Extremely rare

ALMORAVID

686

686   **Abu Bakr b. 'Umar (448-480h)**, AV Dinar

$1000

687   689

687   **Yusuf b. Tashfin (480-500h)**, AV Dinar

688   - AV ¼-Dinar

689   - AR Qirat

$800
$250
$125

690   692

690   **'Ali b. Yusuf (500-537h)**, AV Dinar

691   - BI Dirham

692   - AR Qirat

693   - AR ½-Qirat

$800
$500
$30
$75

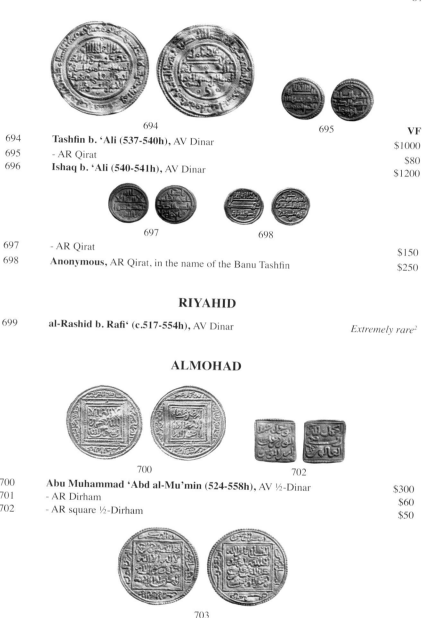

		VF
694	**Tashfin b. 'Ali (537-540h),** AV Dinar	$1000
695	- AR Qirat	$80
696	**Ishaq b. 'Ali (540-541h),** AV Dinar	$1200
697	- AR Qirat	$150
698	**Anonymous,** AR Qirat, in the name of the Banu Tashfin	$250

RIYAHID

699	**al-Rashid b. Rafi' (c.517-554h),** AV Dinar	*Extremely rare[2]*

ALMOHAD

700	**Abu Muhammad 'Abd al-Mu'min (524-558h),** AV ½-Dinar	$300
701	- AR Dirham	$60
702	- AR square ½-Dirham	$50

703	**Abu Ya'qub Yusuf I (558-580h),** AV ½-Dinar	$300

704

704 **Abu Yusuf Ya'qub (580-595h),** AV Dinar $600

705

705 **Abu 'Abd Allah Muhammad (595-610h),** AV Dinar $800
706 **Abu Ya'qub Yusuf II (610-620h),** AV Dinar $1500
707 **Abu Zakariya Yahya (624-633h),** AV Dinar $1500
708 **Abu'l-'Ula Idris I (624-629h),** AV Dinar $1500
709 **Abu Muhammad 'Abd al-Wahid II (630-640h),** AV Dinar $1500
710 **Abu'l-Hasan 'Ali (640-646h),** AV Dinar $1500

711

711 **Abu Hafs 'Umar (646-665h),** AV Dinar $600
712 - AR square Dirham $150
713 **Abu'l-'Ula Idris II (665-668h),** AV Dinar $1000
714 - AV ¼-Dinar $500

715 716

715 **Anonymous,** AR square Dirham, with mintname $50
716 - AR square Dirham, no mint $20

HAFSID

717

717 **Abu Zakariya' Yahya I (627-647h)**, AV Dinar

VF
$1000

718

718 - AV ½-Dinar $300
719 - AV ¼-Dinar $300

720

720 **Abu 'Abd Allah Muhammad I (647-675h)**, AV Dinar

$800

721

721 - AV ½-Dinar $400
722 - AV 1/8-Dinar $150
723 **Abu Zakariya' Yahya II (675-678h)**, AV Dinar *Extremely rare*
724 **Abu Ishaq Ibrahim I (678-681h)**, AV Dinar $2500
725 **Abu Hafs 'Umar I (683-694h)**, AV Dinar $1000
726 **Abu 'Abd Allah Muhammad II (694-709h)**, AV Dinar $1200

727

		VF
727	**Abu Yahya Abu Bakr II (710-747h),** AV Dinar	$600
728	- AV ½-Dinar	$400
729	- AV ¼-Dinar	$300
730	**Abu'l-'Abbas al-Fadl (749-751h),** AV Dinar	$1000
731	**Abu Ishaq Ibrahim II (751-770h),** AV Dinar	$1200
732	**Abu'l-'Abbas Ahmad II (755-758, 761-796h),** AV Dinar	$800
733	**Abu Faris 'Abd al-'Aziz II (796-837h),** AV Dinar	$500

734

734	- AV ½-Dinar	$250
735	**Abu 'Amr 'Uthman (839-893h),** AV Dinar	$500

736

736	- AV ½-Dinar	$400

737

737	**Abu 'Abd Allah Muhammad V (899-932h),** AV ¼-Dinar	$400
738	**Abu'l-'Abbas Ahmad III (948-977h),** AR square Dirham	$150
739	**Anonymous,** AR square Dirham	$100

ZIYANID

		VF
740	**Abu Hammu Musa I (707-718h)**, AV Dinar	$1500

741

741	**Abu Tashufin 'Abd al-Rahman I (718-737h)**, AV Dinar	$800
742	**Abu Hammu Musa II (760-791h)**, AV Dinar	$1500
743	**Abu Ziyan Muhammad II (796-802h)**, AV Dinar	$1500
744	**Abu 'Abd Allah Muhammad III (804-813h)**, AV Dinar	$1500
745	**Abu Malik 'Abd al-Wahid (814-827, 831-833h)**, AV Dinar	$1200

746

| 746 | **Abu 'Abd Allah Muhammad IV (827-831, 833-834h)**, AV Dinar | $1000 |

747

747	- AV ½-Dinar	$600
748	**Abu'l-'Abbas Ahmad I (834-866h)**, AV Dinar	$1500
749	**Abu Hammu Musa III (932-934h)**, AV Dinar	$1500
750	**Abu Muhammad 'Abd Allah II (934-947h)**, AV Dinar	$3000
751	**Abu 'Abd Allah Muhammad VIII (947-950h)**, AV Dinar	$5000
752	**Abu'l-'Abbas Ahmad III (949, 950-957h)**, AV Dinar	$5000

MERINID

753

VF

753	***temp*. Abu Yahya Abu Bakr (642-656h)**, AV Dinar	$600
754	- AV ½-Dinar	$400
755	- AV ¼-Dinar	$200

756

756	- AV 1/8-Dinar	$300
757	**Abu Yusuf Ya'qub (656-685h)**, AV Dinar	$1500

758

758	***temp*. Abu Ya'qub Yusuf (685-706h)**, AV Dinar	$800
759	**Abu Sa'id 'Uthman II (710-731h)**, AV Dinar	$800
760	- AV ½-Dinar	$500
761	***temp*. Abu'l-Hasan 'Ali (731-752h)**, AV Dinar	$800
762	- AV ½-Dinar	$300

763

763	**Abu 'Inan Faris (749-759h)**, AV Dinar	$1000
764	**Abu Ziyan Muhammad III (763-767h)**, AV Dinar	$1200

		VF
765	**Abu Faris 'Abd al-'Aziz I (768-774h)**, AV Dinar	$1200
766	**Abu'l-'Abbas Ahmad (775-786, 789-796h)**, AV Dinar	$1000
767	**Abu Zayd 'Abd al-Rahman (776-784h)**, AV Dinar	$1200
768	- AV ½-Dinar	$600
769	**Abu Faris 'Abd al-'Aziz II (796-799h)**, AV Dinar	$1000
770	- AV ½-Dinar	$300
771	**Abu Sa'id 'Uthman III (800-823h)**, AV Dinar	$600
772	- AV ½-Dinar	$300
773	**Anonymous,** AR square Dirham	$100

WATTASID

774	**Muhammad I al-Shaykh (876-910h)**, AR square ¼-Dirham	$100
775	**Muhammad II al-Burtuqali (910-932h)**, AR square ¼-Dirham	$100
776	**Abu'l-Hasan 'Ali (932-961h)**, AR square Dirham	$150
777	**Abu'l-'Abbas Ahmad (932-952, 954-956h)**, AR square Dirham	$150
778	**Nasir al-din Muhammad III (952-956h)**, AR square ¼-Dirham	$100

EGYPT & SYRIA

Ahmad b. Tulun was an Abbasid governor of Egypt who was able to assert his independence from Baghdad and found the dynasty which bears his name. Tulunid control of Egypt was relatively short-lived, however, and Egypt was recaptured by the Abbasids in 292h. Forty years later, the fall of the caliphate meant that power in Egypt passed to the last Abbasid governor, Muhammad al-Ikhshid. His dynasty was also short-lived and in 358h Egypt fell to the Fatimids, a dynasty originally founded over fifty years earlier in what is now Tunisia. The Fatimids were the first of the three great dynasties who would rule Egypt and much of Syria and the Levant for the next 550 years. During the early period of Fatimid rule in Egypt various minor dynasties ruled parts of Syria, but they gradually disappeared as Fatimid influence increased. The Fatimids were succeeded by the Ayyubids, who were in turn succeeded by the Mamluks. Mamluk rule came to an end with their defeat by the Ottomans in 922h.

TULUNID

Grabar, O., *The Coinage of the Tulunids,* ANS Numismatic Notes and Monographs No. 139, New York, 1957

779

		VF
779	**Ahmad b. Tulun (254-270h),** AV Dinar (common mint: Misr)	$500
780	- Æ Fals, cast	$300

781

781	- Æ Fals, anonymous, struck	$250

782

782	**Khumarawayh b. Ahmad (270-282h),** AV Dinar (common mint: Misr)	$400
783	- AV Dinar, donative type, small flan	*Extremely rare[1]*

---

[1]   Baldwin's Islamic Coin Auction 24, 9 May 2013, lot 4559

784

		VF
784	- AR Dirham	$400
785	**Jaysh b. Khumarawayh (282-283h)**, AV Dinar	$4000

786

786	**Harun b. Khumarawayh (283-292h)**, AV Dinar (common mint: Misr)	$400
787	- AR Dirham	$500
788	**Ibrahim b. Khumarawayh (292h)**, AR Dirham	*Extremely rare[2]*

AMIRS OF CRETE

Miles, G.C., *The Coinage of the Arab Amirs of Crete*, ANS Numismatic Notes and Monographs No. 160, New York, 1970

789

789	**Shu'ayb b. 'Umar (fl.270-281h)**, AV Dinar	$20,000

790

790	- Æ Fals	$400
791	**Muhammad b. Shu'ayb (c.300h)**, Æ Fals	$500

---

[2] Baldwin's Islamic Coin Auction 21, 17 July 2012, lot 367

IKHSHIDID

Bacharach, J.L., *Islamic History through Coins: An Analysis and Catalogue of Tenth-Century Ikhshidid Coinage*, Cairo, 2006

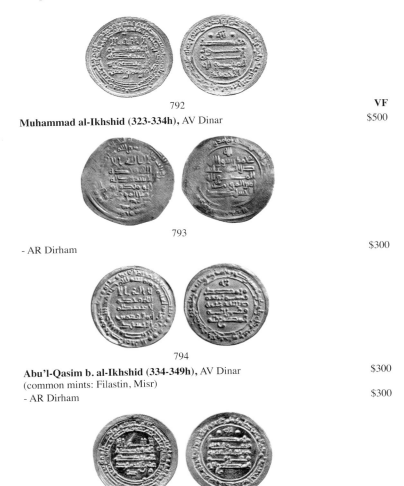

792

		VF
792	**Muhammad al-Ikhshid (323-334h),** AV Dinar	$500

793

| 793 | - AR Dirham | $300 |

794

| 794 | **Abu'l-Qasim b. al-Ikhshid (334-349h),** AV Dinar (common mints: Filastin, Misr) | $300 |
| 795 | - AR Dirham | $300 |

796

796	**'Ali b. al-Ikhshid (349-355h),** AV Dinar	$400
797	- AR Dirham	$150
798	**Kafur (355-357h),** AV Dinar	$500

799

		VF
799	**Ahmad b. 'Ali (357-358h),** AV Dinar	$800
800	- AR Dirham	$400

QARMATID

Vardanyan, A., 'From Sectarians to Politicians: Twelve Years of Qarmatid Military Activity in Syria, Palestine and West Arabia (357-368 / 967-978)', *Revue Numismatique,* 2011

801	**Anonymous,** AV Dinar, in the name of the Chief Sayyids	$12,000
802	- AR Dirham	$1200

803

803	**al-Hasan b. Ahmad (fl.361-364h),** AV Dinar	$8000
804	- AR Dirham	$1200

805

805	**Abu Mansur al-Mu'izzi (fl.364-367),** AV Dinar	$10,000
806	- AR Dirham	$600

FATIMID

Nicol, N.D., *A Corpus of Fatimid Coins,* Trieste, 2006

807

807	**al-Mahdi (297-322h),** AV Dinar	$1200

	808	809	**VF**

808	- AV ¼-Dinar	$400
809	- AR Dirham	$1000
810	- AR ½-Dirham	$500

811

811	**al-Qa'im (322-334h),** AV Dinar	$1200
812	- AV ¼-Dinar	$800
813	- AR ½-Dirham	$300

814

| 814 | **Abu Yazid Makhlad, rebel (333-334h),** AV Dinar | $5000 |

815   816

815	**al-Mansur (334-341h),** AV Dinar	$1500
816	- AV ¼-Dinar	$800
817	- AV 1/8-Dinar	$800
818	- AR ½-Dirham	*Extremely rare*

819

| 819 | **al-Mu'izz (341-365h),** AV Dinar | $250 |
| | (common mints: Misr, al-Mansuriya) | |

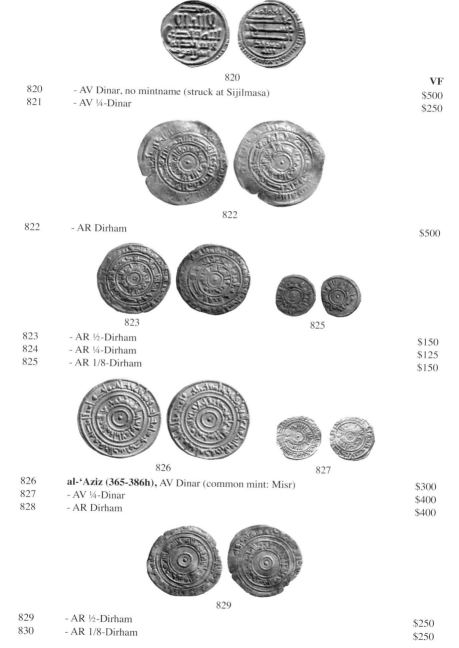

820

820	- AV Dinar, no mintname (struck at Sijilmasa) — $500
821	- AV ¼-Dinar — $250

822

822	- AR Dirham — $500

823   825

823	- AR ½-Dirham — $150
824	- AR ¼-Dirham — $125
825	- AR 1/8-Dirham — $150

826   827

826	**al-'Aziz (365-386h),** AV Dinar (common mint: Misr) — $300
827	- AV ¼-Dinar — $400
828	- AR Dirham — $400

829

829	- AR ½-Dirham — $250
830	- AR 1/8-Dirham — $250

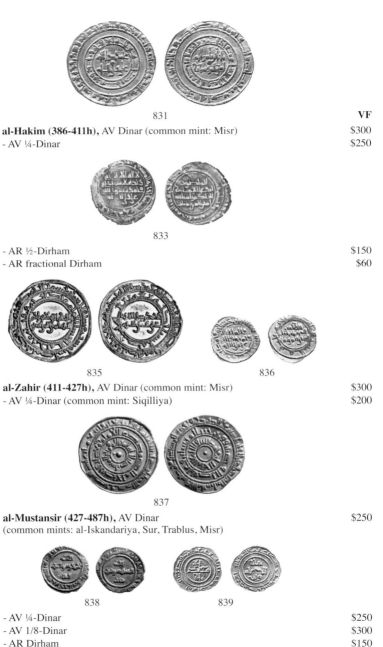

	831	**VF**
831	**al-Hakim (386-411h),** AV Dinar (common mint: Misr)	$300
832	- AV ¼-Dinar	$250

833

833	- AR ½-Dirham	$150
834	- AR fractional Dirham	$60

835   836

835	**al-Zahir (411-427h),** AV Dinar (common mint: Misr)	$300
836	- AV ¼-Dinar (common mint: Siqilliya)	$200

837

837	**al-Mustansir (427-487h),** AV Dinar	$250
	(common mints: al-Iskandariya, Sur, Trablus, Misr)	

838   839

838	- AV ¼-Dinar	$250
839	- AV 1/8-Dinar	$300
840	- AR Dirham	$150
841	- BI Dirham Aswad	$150

842

842   *temp.* **al-Basasiri (450-451h)**, AV Dinar, in the name of al-Mustansir   **VF**
$7500

843

843   **al-Musta'li (487-495h)**, AV Dinar $1000
844   - AV ¼-Dinar $500
845   - BI Dirham Aswad $100

846

846   **al-Amir (495-524h)**, AV Dinar $300
        (common mints: al-Iskandariya, Misr)
847   - AV ¼-Dinar $400
848   - AR Dirham   *Extremely rare*
849   **Interregnum (524-526h)**, AV Dinar, in the name of al-Muntazar $6000

850

850   **al-Hafiz (526-544h)**, AV Dinar $600

851

851   **al-Zafir (544-549h)**, AV Dinar $1500

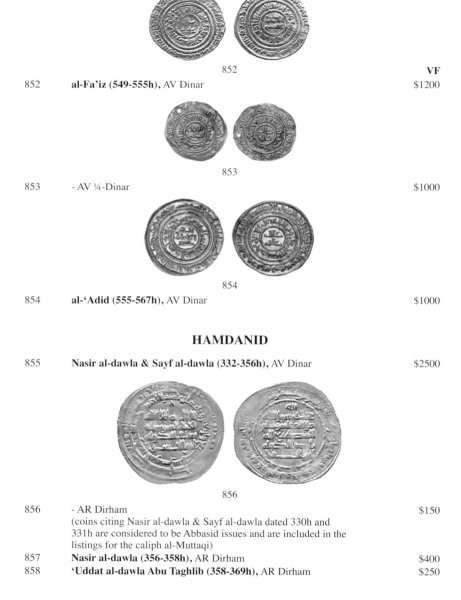

	852	**VF**
852	**al-Fa'iz (549-555h)**, AV Dinar	$1200
	853	
853	- AV ¼-Dinar	$1000
	854	
854	**al-'Adid (555-567h)**, AV Dinar	$1000

HAMDANID

| 855 | **Nasir al-dawla & Sayf al-dawla (332-356h)**, AV Dinar | $2500 |

856

| 856 | - AR Dirham | $150 |

(coins citing Nasir al-dawla & Sayf al-dawla dated 330h and
331h are considered to be Abbasid issues and are included in the
listings for the caliph al-Muttaqi)

| 857 | **Nasir al-dawla (356-358h)**, AR Dirham | $400 |
| 858 | **'Uddat al-dawla Abu Taghlib (358-369h)**, AR Dirham | $250 |

ANTI-HAMDANID REVOLT

859 **Anonymous,** AR Dirham, in the name of the caliph al-Muti'

'UQAYLID

860

860 **Muhammad b. al-Musayyib (c.380-385h),** AR Dirham $250

861

861 **Janah al-dawla 'Ali (385-390h),** AR Dirham $250
862 **Husam al-dawla al-Muqallad (385-391h),** AR Dirham $150
863 **Sinan al-dawla al-Hasan (390-393h),** AR Dirham $250
864 **Nur al-dawla Abu Mus'ab (393-396h),** AR Dirham $300

865

865 **Mu'tamid al-dawla Abu'l-Muni' (391-442h),** AR Dirham $150
866 **Abu'l-Fadl (fl.405-409h),** AR Dirham $150

867

867 **Mu'tamid al-dawla & Abu'l-Fadl (c.410-411h),** AR Dirham $125

VF

868   **Muzahir al-dawla (fl.399-424h)**, AR Dirham $300

869

869   **Kamal al-dawla Gharib (401-425h)**, AR Dirham $300

870   **Najdat al-dawla (fl.405h)**, AR Dirham   *Extremely rare[3]*

MARWANID

871   **al-Hasan b. Marwan (380-387h)**, AR Dirham $250

872

872   **Sa'id b. Marwan (387-401h)**, AR Dirham $200

873

873   **Nasr al-dawla Abu Nasr (401-453h)**, AR Dirham $150

MIRDASID

874

874   **Asad al-dawla Salih (414-420h)**, AV Dinar $7500

---

3   Stephen Album Rare Coins, Auction 9, 11 December 2010, lot 50

875

		VF
875	**Shibl al-dawla Nasr I (420-429h),** AV Dinar	$4000
876	- AR Dirham	$100

NUMAYRID

877	**Sani'at al-dawla Shabib (410-431h),** BI Dirham	$500

SELJUQ OF SYRIA

878	**Ridwan b. Tutush (488-507h),** BI Dirham	$250
879	**Anonymous,** Æ Fals	$75

BURID

880	**Tughtekin (497-522h),** BI Dirham	$500
881	- Æ Dirham	$800

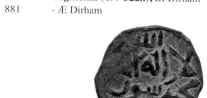

882

882	**Taj al-Muluk Buri (522-526h),** Æ Qirtas	$500
883	**Shihab al-din Mahmud (529-533h),** AV Dinar	$10,000
884	**Abaq (534-549h),** AV Dinar	$10,000
885	- AV ¼-Dinar	$750
886	- BI Dirham	$150

SICILY

887

887   **Muhammad b. 'Abbad (616-619h),** BI Dirham

AYYUBID

Balog, P., *The Coinage of the Ayyubids,* London, 1980

888

888   **al-Nasir Salah al-din Yusuf, 'Saladin' (567-589h),** AV Dinar, in the name of Mahmud b. Zengi

$2000

889

889   - AV Dinar, citing caliph al-Mustadi

$800

890

890   - AV Dinar, citing caliph al-Nasir

$500

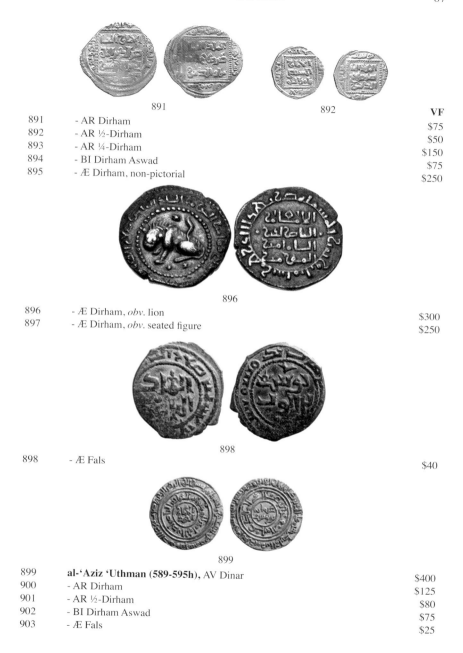

		VF
891	- AR Dirham	$75
892	- AR ½-Dirham	$50
893	- AR ¼-Dirham	$150
894	- BI Dirham Aswad	$75
895	- Æ Dirham, non-pictorial	$250
896	- Æ Dirham, *obv.* lion	$300
897	- Æ Dirham, *obv.* seated figure	$250
898	- Æ Fals	$40
899	**al-'Aziz 'Uthman (589-595h),** AV Dinar	$400
900	- AR Dirham	$125
901	- AR ½-Dirham	$80
902	- BI Dirham Aswad	$75
903	- Æ Fals	$25

904

904	**al-Mansur Muhammad (595-596h)**, AV Dinar	$600
905	**al-'Adil Abu Bakr I (596-615h)**, AV Dinar	$300

906

906	- AR Dirham	$40
907	- AR ½-Dirham	$50
908	- Æ Dirham, *obv.* facing bust	$150
909	- Æ Fals	$25

910

910	**al-Kamil Muhammad I (615-635h)**, AV Dinar	$250

911   914

911	- AR Dirham	$30
912	- AR ½-Dirham	$50
913	- BI Dirham Aswad	$60
914	- Æ Fals	$40

915

VF

915   **al-'Adil Abu Bakr II (635-637h)**, AV Dinar $500

916

916   - AR Dirham $60
917   - AR ½-Dirham $50

918   919

918   **al-Salih Ayyub (637-647h)**, AV Dinar $500
919   - AV ½-Dinar $400
920   - AR Dirham $80
921   - AR ½-Dirham $60
922   - Æ Fals $40
923   **al-Mu'azzam Turanshah IV (647-648h)**, AR Dirham $250
924   **al-Ashraf Musa (648-652h)**, AV Dinar $1500

AYYUBID OF ALEPPO

925   926

925   **al-Zahir Ghazi (582-613h)**, AR Dirham $40
926   - AR ½-Dirham $40

927

927   - Æ Fals $30

928

928   **al-'Aziz Muhammad (613-634h)**, AR Dirham $100
929   - AR ½-Dirham $75
930   - Æ Fals $30

931

931   **al-Nasir Yusuf II (634-658h)**, AR Dirham $30
932   - AR ½-Dirham $40
933   - Æ Fals $30

AYYUBID OF DAMASCUS

934   **al-Afdal 'Ali (589-592h)**, AR Dirham $125
935   **al-Salih Isma'il (635, 637-643h)**, AR Dirham $40
936   - AR ½-Dirham $30

AYYUBID OF HAMAH

937   **al-Mansur Muhammad I (587-617h)**, Æ Dirham, *obv.* seated $250
         figure
938   - Æ Fals $50
939   **al-Muzaffar Mahmud (626-642h)**, Æ Fals $75
940   **al-Mansur Muhammad II (642-683h)**, Æ Fals $50

AYYUBID OF AL-JAZIRA

941

		VF
941	**al-Awhad Ayyub (596-607h),** Æ Dirham, *obv.* facing bust	$200
942	**al-Ashraf Musa (607-617h),** AR Dirham	$125
943	- Æ Dirham, *obv.* seated figure	$150
944	**al-Muzaffar Ghazi (617-642h),** Æ Fals	$50
945	**al-Kamil Muhammad II (642-658h),** AR Dirham	*Extremely rare*
946	- Æ Fals	$75

AYYUBID OF HISN KAYFA

947	**al-Muwahhid 'Abd Allah (647-659h),** AR Dirham, citing Hulagu	$250
948	**al-'Adil Sulayman (780-828h),** AR Tanka	$250
949	**al-Ashraf Ahmad (828-836h),** AR Tanka	$250
950	**al-Kamil Khalil I (836-852h),** AR Tanka	$250
951	**al-Zahir Khalil II (fl.910s h),** AR Tanka	$125
952	- AR ½-Tanka	$175

MAMLUK

Balog, P., *The Coinage of the Mamluk Sultans of Egypt and Syria,* ANS Numismatic Studies No. 12, New York, 1964

953
954

953	**al-Mu'izz Aybak (648-655h),** AV Dinar	$2500
954	- AR Dirham	$125

955

955	**al-Mansur 'Ali I (655-657h)**, AV Dinar	$1000
956	- AR Dirham	$75

957

957	**al-Muzaffar Qutuz (657-658h)**, AV Dinar	$1500
958	- AR Dirham	$75

959

959	**al-Zahir Baybars I (658-676h)**, AV Dinar	$500

960

960	- AR Dirham	$40
961	- AR fractional Dirham	$25
962	- Æ Fals	$25

963

963	**al-Sa'id Baraka Qan (676-678h)**, AV Dinar	$4000
964	- AR Dirham	$75
965	**al-'Adil Salamish (678h)**, AR Dirham	$125

966   967   **VF**

966	**al-Mansur Qala'un (678-689h),** AV Dinar	$500
967	- AR Dirham	$30
968	- Æ Fals	$50
969	**al-Ashraf Khalil (689-693h),** AV Dinar	$800
970	- AR Dirham	$75
971	**al-Nasir Muhammad I, 1ˢᵗ reign (693-694h),** AV Dinar	*Extremely rare*
972	**al-'Adil Kitbugha (694-696h),** AV Dinar	$800
973	- AR Dirham	$75

974

974	**al-Mansur Lajin (696-698h),** AV Dinar	$600
975	- AR Dirham	$75
976	**al-Nasir Muhammad I, 2ⁿᵈ reign (698-708h),** AV Dinar	$600
977	**al-Muzaffar Baybars II (708-709h),** AV Dinar	*Extremely rare*
978	- AR Dirham	$125
979	- Æ Fals	$50

980   981

980	**al-Nasir Muhammad I, 3ʳᵈ reign (709-741h),** AV Dinar	$500
981	- AR Dirham	$30
982	- Æ Fals	$30
983	**al-Mansur Abu Bakr (741-742h),** AV Dinar	$10,000
984	- Æ Fals, anonymous	$50

985   **VF**

985	**al-Ashraf Kujuk (742h),** AV Dinar	$8000
986	**al-Nasir Ahmad I (742-743h),** AV Dinar	$10,000
987	- AR Dirham	$125
988	**al-Salih Isma'il (743-746h),** AV Dinar	$3000
989	- AR Dirham	$75

990

990	- Æ Fals	$30
991	**al-Kamil Sha'ban I (746-747h),** AV Dinar	$2500
992	- AR Dirham	$125
993	**al-Muzaffar Hajji I (747-748h),** AV Dinar	$1500
994	- AR Dirham	$125
995	- Æ Fals	$50

996   998

996	**al-Nasir Hasan, 1st reign (748-752h),** AV Dinar	$500
997	- AR Dirham	$75
998	- Æ Fals	$30

999

999	**al-Salih Salih (752-755h),** AV Dinar	$1200
1000	- Æ Fals	$30

1001

VF

1001	**al-Nasir Hasan, 2nd reign (755-762h),** AV Dinar	$500
1002	- AR Dirham	$75
1003	- Æ Fals	$30

1004

1004	**al-Mansur Muhammad II (762-764h),** AV Dinar	$800
1005	- AR Dirham	$125
1006	- Æ Fals	$30

1007   1009

1007	**al-Ashraf Sha'ban II (764-778h),** AV Dinar	$500
1008	- AR Dirham	$30
1009	- Æ Fals	$25

1010   1012

1010	**al-Mansur 'Ali II (778-783h),** AV Dinar	$600
1011	- AR Dirham	$75
1012	- Æ Fals	$25

1013

		VF
1013	**al-Salih Hajji II, 1st reign (783-784h),** AV Dinar	$500
1014	- AR Dirham	$125
1015	- Æ Wuqiya	$800
1016	- Æ Fals	$50

1017

1017	**al-Zahir Barquq, 1st reign (784-791h),** AV Dinar	$500
1018	- AR Dirham	$25
1019	- Æ Fals	$25
1020	**al-Mansur Hajji II, 2nd reign (791-792h),** AV Dinar	$2000
1021	- AR Dirham	$125
1022	- Æ Fals	$50

1023

1023	**al-Zahir Barquq, 2nd reign (792-801h),** AV Dinar	$500
1024	- AR Dirham	$25

1025

1025	- Æ Fals	$25
1026	**al-Nasir Faraj, 1st reign (801-808h),** AV Dinar	$500
1027	- Æ Fals	$25
1028	**al-Nasir Faraj, 2nd reign (809-815h),** AV Dinar	$500

1029

| 1029 | - AV Bunduqi | $300 |

1030

| 1030 | **al-Musta'in, caliph (815h),** AV Bunduqi | $1200 |
| 1031 | - AR Dirham | $125 |

1032

| 1032 | **al-Mu'ayyad Shaykh (815-824h),** AV Dinar | $1500 |

1033   1034

1033	- AV Mithqal	$1200
1034	- AV Bunduqi	$300
1035	- AR Dirham	$125
1036	- AR ½-Dirham	$75
1037	- AR ¼-Dirham	$60
1038	**al-Muzaffar Ahmad II (824h),** AR ½-Dirham	$150
1039	**al-Salih Muhammad III (824-825h),** AR ½-Dirham	$150

1040

| 1040 | **al-Ashraf Barsbay (825-841h),** AV Ashrafi | $150 |
| 1041 | - AR Dirham | $25 |

		VF
1042	- AR ¾-Dirham	$75
1043	- AR ½-Dirham	$50
1044	- AR 3/8-Dirham	$40

1045

| 1045 | **al-'Aziz Yusuf (841-842h),** AV Ashrafi | $800 |

1046   1047

1046	**al-Zahir Jaqmaq (842-857h),** AV Ashrafi	$150
1047	- AR Dirham	$25
1048	- Æ Fals	$40

1049

| 1049 | **al-Mansur 'Uthman (857h),** AV Ashrafi | $1500 |

1050   1051   1052

1050	**al-Ashraf Aynal (857-865h),** AV Ashrafi	$150
1051	- AR Dirham	$25
1052	- AR ½-Dirham	$75
1053	- Æ Fals	$40
1054	**al-Mu'ayyad Ahmad III (865h),** AV Ashrafi	$800
1055	- AR Dirham	$75
1056	**al-Zahir Khushqadam (865-872h),** AV Ashrafi	$150

1057   1058

| 1057 | - AR Dirham | $25 |
| 1058 | - Æ Fals | $40 |

VF

1059	**al-Zahir Bilbay (872h)**, AV Ashrafi	$3000
1060	**al-Zahir Timurbugha (872-873h)**, AV Ashrafi	$1500
1061	- Æ Fals	$75

1062

1062	**al-Ashraf Qa'itbay (873-901h)**, AV Ashrafi	$150
1063	- AR Dirham	$25
1064	- AR ½-Dirham	$60
1065	- Æ Fals	$40
1066	**al-Nasir Muhammad IV (901-904h)**, AV Ashrafi	$600
1067	- AR Dirham	$40

1068

1068	- Æ Fals	$50
1069	**al-Zahir Qansuh I (904-905h)**, AV Ashrafi	$500
1070	**al-Ashraf Janbalat (905-906h)**, AV Ashrafi	$10,000
1071	**al-'Adil Tumanbay I (906h)**, AV Ashrafi	$800

1072

1072	**al-Ashraf Qansuh II (906-922h)**, AV Ashrafi	$250
1073	- AR Dirham	$25
1074	- Æ Fals	$40

1075

1075	**al-Ashraf Tumanbay II (922h)**, AV Ashrafi	$3000
1076	**Anonymous,** Æ Fals, various types	$25

ARABIAN PENINSULA & EAST AFRICA

Nearly all the coinage of the Arabian peninsula during the period covered by this volume was struck in the Yemen and Oman. Abbasid control over these areas had effectively disappeared by the end of the 3rd century AH. In the Yemen the Rassids were the first dynasty to come to prominence; they and various other minor dynasties ruled for the next two centuries until the Ayyubid conquest of much of the Yemen in 569-570h. After the fall of the Ayyubids power passed to the most important and longest-lasting of the Yemeni dynasties of this period, the Rasulids. The Rasulid dynasty lasted until the early 9th century AH, after which virtually no coinage was struck in the Yemen for around a century. In the late 3rd century AH coins began to be struck by the local governors of Oman; these governors were succeeded by the Wajihids, who ruled until the conquest of Oman by the Buwayhids in the mid-4th century AH. The only coins issued by local rulers in Oman after this time are a series of gold dinars struck by the Mukramids, who ruled for a brief period at the beginning of the 5th century AH. In the mid-5th century AH Oman began to decline in importance and virtually no coinage is known for the rest of this period.

During the 8th-10th centuries AH a series of (mostly copper) coins were issued by many local Islamic rulers in East Africa. Little is known about most of these rulers; their dates cannot be accurately determined at present (the coins provide little help here as they are almost always undated).

Album, S., *Sylloge of Islamic Coins in the Ashmolean, Volume 10: Arabia and East Africa*, Oxford, 1999
Darley-Doran, R.E., *History of Currency in the Sultanate of Oman*, Muscat, 1990

BANU MISMAR

1077

		VF
1077	**Mismar b. Salm (fl.273h)**, BI Dirham	$200

RASSID (1st period)

1078

1078	**al-Hadi (284-298h)**, AV Dinar	$400
1079	- AR Dirham	$2500
1080	- AR Sudaysi	$40
1081	**Muhammad b. al-Qasim (c.300h)**, AR Sudaysi	$150
1082	**al-Nasir (301-325h)**, AR ½-Dirham	*Extremely rare[1]*

[1] Stephen Album Rare Coins, Auction 16, 17-18 May 2013, lot 265

1083

1083	- AR Sudaysi	$20

1084

1084	**al-Mansur al-Qasim (389-393h),** AV Dinar	$3000
1085	- AR Sudaysi	$250
1086	**al-Mahdi al-Husayn (393-404h),** AR Sudaysi	$125

FATIMID PARTISANS

1087	**Anonymous,** AR Sudaysi, in the name of al-Mahdi	$150

AMIRS OF 'ATHAR

1088	**Muhammad b. al-Qasim (fl.346-359h),** AV Dinar	$2500

1089

1089	**'Ali b. Muhammad (fl.362-370h),** AV Dinar	$2500
1090	**al-Samu b. Muhammad (fl.373-374h),** AV Dinar	$2500
1091	**al-Mu'ammar b. Muhammad (fl.379h),** AV Dinar	$2500
1092	**al-Mansur b. Muhammad (fl.379h),** AV Dinar	$2500

TARAFID

1093   VF

1093	al-Faraj al-Tarafi (fl.381-392h), AV Dinar	$1500
1094	Bushri b. 'Abd Allah (fl.393-394h), AV Dinar	$2500

ZIYADID

1095

1095	Ishaq b. Ibrahim (343-362h), AV Dinar	$1200
1096	- AR Sudaysi	*Extremely rare*
1097	'Ali b. Ibrahim (362-370h), AV Dinar	*Extremely rare*

1098

1098	al-Muzaffar b. 'Ali (c.370-435h), AV Dinar	$400

1099

1099	'Ali b. al-Muzaffar (fl.434-442h), AV Dinar	$300

NAJJAHID

1100

		VF
1100	**Jayyash b. al-Mu'ayyad (fl.465h)**, AV Dinar	$400
1101	**al-Fatik II b. al-Mansur (c.520-531h)**, AV Dinar	$650

KHAWLANID

1102	**Yahya b. Abi Hashid (fl.438h)**, AV Dinar	$650

SULAYHID

1103

1103	**'Ali b. Muhammad (439-473h)**, AV Dinar	$300

1104

1104	**al-Mukarram Ahmad (473-484h)**, AV Dinar	$250
1105	- AV ½-Dinar	$250

1106 1107

1106	*temp.* **'Arwa bint Ahmad (484-532h)**, AV Dinar, in the name of al-Mukarram Ahmad	$200
1107	- AV ½-Dinar, in the name of al-Mukarram Ahmad	$150

ZURAY'ID

1108

1108	**Anonymous,** AV Dinar, in the name of the deceased Sulayhid ruler al-Mukarram Ahmad	$300

1109

1109	**Anonymous,** AV ½-Dinar, citing the Fatimid caliph al-Amir	$500
1110	**Muhammad b. Saba' (534-550h),** AV Dinar	$400

1111

1111	**'Imran b. Muhammad (550-561h),** AV Dinar	$600

MAHDID OF ZABID

1112	*temp.* **'Abd al-Nabi b. 'Ali (558-569h),** AR Dirham	$150

RASSID (2ⁿᵈ period)

1113

1113	**al-Mansur 'Abd Allah (583-614h),** AR Dirham	$150
1114	**al-Mutawakkil Ahmad (623-656h),** AR Dirham	$250

1115

		VF
1115	**al-Mahdi Ahmad (646-656h)**, AR Dirham	$150
1116	**al-Nasir Muhammad (773-793h)**, AR Dirham	$300

AYYUBID OF THE YEMEN

1117	**al-Mu'azzam Turanshah (569-575h)**, AV Dinar	$1200
1118	- AR Dirham	$300
1119	**al-Nasir Salah al-din Yusuf (575-589h)**, AR Dirham	$150
1120	**al-'Aziz Tughtekin (579-593h)**, AV Dinar	*Extremely rare*

1121

1121	- AR ½-Dirham	$300
1122	**al-Mu'izz Isma'il (593-598h)**, AR Dirham	$100
1123	- Æ Fals	$400

1124

1124	**al-Nasir Ayyub (598-611h)**, AR Dirham	$75
1125	**al-Mas'ud Yusuf (612-626h)**, AR Dirham	$125
1126	**al-Kamil Muhammad I (626-627, 631-634h)**, AR Dirham	$250

1127

1127	**al-'Adil Abu Bakr (627-631h)**, AR Dirham	$250

RASULID

1128 **al-Mansur 'Umar I (626-647h),** AV Dinar *Extremely rare*

	1129		1130

1129 - AR Dirham $80
1130 - Æ Fals $100

1131

1131 **al-Muzaffar Yusuf (647-694h),** AR Dirham $30

1132

1132 **al-Ashraf 'Umar II (694-696h),** AR Dirham $300
1133 **al-Mu'ayyad Da'ud (696-721h),** AV Dinar $4000
1134 - AR Dirham $50

1135

1135 **al-Mansur Ayyub, rebel (c.721-722h),** AR Dirham $400
1136 **al-Mujahid 'Ali (721-764h),** AV Dinar *Extremely rare*

1137

| | | | VF |
|1137| - AR Dirham | | $65 |

1138

| 1138 | **al-Afdal al-'Abbas (764-778h),** AR Dirham | $50 |

1139

1139	**al-Ashraf Isma'il I (778-803h),** AR Dirham	$80
1140	**al-Nasir Ahmad (803-827h),** AR Dirham	$50
1141	**al-Ashraf Isma'il II (830-831h),** AR Dirham	$300
1142	**al-Zahir Yahya (831-842h),** AV Dinar	*Extremely rare*
1143	- AR Dirham	$600

HUSAYNID SHARIFS

1144

| 1144 | **Muhammad b. Mika'il (763-765h),** AR Dirham | $150 |

TAHIRID

		VF
1145	**'Amir b. Da'ud (923-945h),** AR Dirham	$100

RASSID (3rd period)

1146	**Sharaf al-din (912-965h),** AR Dirham	$65
1147	- Æ Fals	$50

GOVERNORS OF OMAN

1148

1148	**Ahmad b. al-Husayn (fl.289h),** AR Dirham	$2500

1149

1149	**Ahmad b. Halil (fl.290-312h),** AR Dirham	$700
1150	**'Abd al-Halim b. Ibrahim (fl.313h),** AR Dirham	$1000

WAJIHID

1151

1151	**Yusuf b. Wajih (314-332h),** AR Dirham	$500

1152

			VF
1152	**Muhammad b. Yusuf (332-340h)**, AR Dirham		$750
1153	**'Umar b. Yusuf (fl.340-350h)**, AR Dirham		$1500

AMIRS OF OMAN

1154   **Hallaj b. Hatim (fl.358-361h)**, AR Dirham   *Extremely rare*

MUKRAMID

1155   **Abu Muhammad Hasan b. Mukram (fl.408-411h)**, AV Dinar $1500

1156

1156   **Nasir al-din (411-427h)**, AV Dinar $800

1157

1157   **Abu'l-Hasan (427-430h)**, AV Dinar $800

1158

1158	**Abu Muhammad II (430h)**, AV Dinar	$1200
1159	*temp.* **'Ali b. Hattal (430-432h)**, AV Dinar	$1200

SULTANS OF MOGADISHU

		VF
1160	**Abu Bakr b. Muhammad (fl.722h)**, BI Dirham	*Extremely rare*
1161	**Zubayr b. 'Umar,** Æ Fals	$200
1162	**'Ali b. Yusuf,** Æ Fals	$150
1163	**Muhammad al-Zafir,** Æ Fals	$250
1164	**Anonymous,** Æ Fals	$150

SULTANS OF KILWA

1165	**'Ali b. al-Hasan,** Æ Fals	$150
1166	**Da'ud b. al-Hasan,** Æ Fals	$250
1167	**al-Hasan b. Sulayman (c.715h),** Æ Fals	$150
1168	**Sulayman b. al-Hasan (fl.732h),** Æ Fals	$125
1169	**Da'ud b. Sulayman,** Æ Fals	$150
1170	**Anonymous,** Æ Fals, imitating Rasulid dirham of al-Nasir Ahmad	$125

SULTANS OF ZANZIBAR

1171	**al-Husayn b. Ahmad,** Æ Fals	$150
1172	**Ishaq b. Hasan,** Æ Fals	$150

AL-JAZIRA & ANATOLIA

The late 5th century AH saw the capture of much of Anatolia from the Byzantine Empire by the Great Seljuqs. The decline of Byzantine influence, coupled with the decline of the Seljuq kingdom in the early 6th century, provided an opportunity for the establishment of various dynasties, mostly of Seljuq origin, in the Jazira and Anatolia. In the Jazira the most important of these were the Artuqids and Zengids. The distinguishing feature of the coinage of these (and related smaller) dynasties is the use of pictorial images on the copper coins; this is very unusual for Islamic coinage. There are a large number of different pictorial types as the designs were changed often, sometimes several times in a single reign. The other major dynasty of this period was the Seljuqs of Rum, who ruled in central Anatolia for a century and a half. The 7th century AH saw the Mongol conquest of the Jazira and most of Anatolia. In western Anatolia a few independent principalities (known as beyliks) were established after the end of Rum Seljuq power; these were all eventually conquered by the Ottomans.

Hennequin, G., *Catalogue des Monnaies Musulmanes de la Bibliothèque Nationale: Asie Pré-Mongole - Les Salguqs et Leurs Successeurs*, Paris, 1985
Spengler, W.F., & Sayles, W.G., *Turkoman Figural Bronze Coins and Their Iconography, Vol. I - The Artuqids*, Lodi, 1992
Spengler, W.F., & Sayles, W.G., *Turkoman Figural Bronze Coins and Their Iconography, Vol. II - The Zengids*, Lodi, 1996

ARTUQID OF HISN KAYFA & AMID

		VF
1173	**Fakhr al-din Qara Arslan (539-570h),** Æ Dirham (SS 1)	$500

1174

| 1174 | - Æ Dirham (SS 2) | $500 |

1175

| 1175 | - Æ Dirham (SS 3) | $1000 |

1176   **VF**
1176   - Æ Dirham (SS 4) $600

1177
1177   - Æ Dirham (SS 5) $1000

1178
1178   - Æ Dirham (SS 6) $250

1179
1179   - Æ Dirham (SS 7) $500

1180

1180   - Æ Dirham (SS 8)

VF
$800

1181

1181   **Nur al-din Muhammad (570-581h),** Æ Dirham (SS 9) $800

1182

1182   - Æ Dirham (SS 10) $600

1183

1183   - Æ Dirham (SS 11) $500

1184

1184   **Qutb al-din Sukman II (581-597h),** Æ Dirham (SS 12)

1185

1185   - Æ Dirham (SS 13)

1186

1186   - Æ Dirham (SS 14)

1187

1187   **Nasir al-din Mahmud (597-619h),** Æ Dirham (SS 15)

VF
$500

$400

$300

$300

1188

1188   - Æ Dirham (SS 16)
1189   - Æ Dirham (SS 17)

VF
$250
$500

1190

1190   - Æ Dirham (SS 18)

$250

1191

1191   **Rukn al-din Mawdud (619-629h),** Æ Dirham (SS 19)
1192   - Æ Fals (SS 20)

$275
$150

ARTUQID OF KHARTABIRT

1193

1193   **'Imad al-din Abu Bakr (581-600h),** Æ Dirham (SS 21)
1194   - Æ Dirham (SS 22)

$1200
$500

1195

		VF
1195	- Æ Dirham (SS 23)	$750

ARTUQID OF MARDIN

1196	**Husam al-din Timurtash (516-547h)**, Æ Dirham (SS 24)	*Extremely rare*
1197	- Æ Dirham (SS 25)	$250

1198

1198	- Æ Dirham (SS 26)	$300

1199

1199	**Najm al-din Alpi (547-572h)**, Æ Dirham, SS 26 with countermark	$150

1200

1200	- Æ Dirham (SS 27)	$250

1201

1201   - Æ Dirham (SS 28)

VF
$275

1202

1202   - Æ Dirham (SS 29)

$250

1203

1203   - Æ Dirham (SS 30)

$200

1204

1204   **Qutb al-din Il-Ghazi II (572-580h),** Æ Dirham (SS 31)

$250

1205   **VF**
1205   - Æ Dirham (SS 32) $150

1206
1206   **Husam al-din Yuluq Arslan (580-597h),** Æ Dirham (SS 33) $250

1207
1207   - Æ Dirham (SS 34) $250

1208
1208   - Æ Dirham (SS 35) $200

1209

VF

1209　　- Æ Dirham (SS 36)　　　　　　　　　　　　　　　$250

1210

1210　　**Nasir al-din Artuq Arslan (597-637h),** AR Dirham　　$125

1211

1211　　- Æ Dirham (SS 37)　　　　　　　　　　　　　　　$250

1212

1212　　- Æ Dirham (SS 38)　　　　　　　　　　　　　　　$300

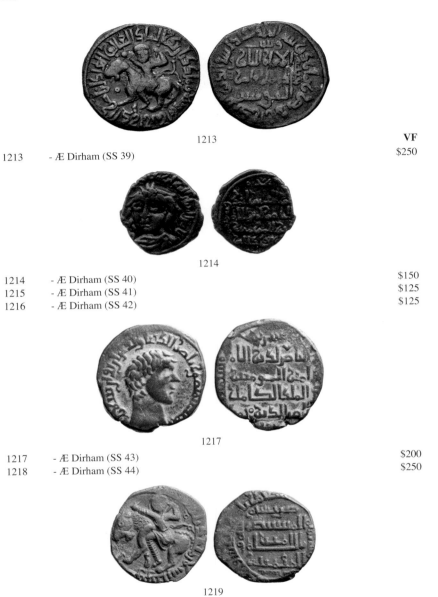

1213

1213   - Æ Dirham (SS 39) $250

1214

1214   - Æ Dirham (SS 40) $150
1215   - Æ Dirham (SS 41) $125
1216   - Æ Dirham (SS 42) $125

1217

1217   - Æ Dirham (SS 43) $200
1218   - Æ Dirham (SS 44) $250

1219

1219   - Æ Dirham (SS 45) $250

1220

VF

| 1220 | - Æ Dirham (SS 46) | $150 |

1221

| 1221 | - Æ Dirham (SS 47) | $300 |

1222

| 1222 | - Æ Dirham (SS 48) | $150 |

1223

| 1223 | **Najm al-din Ghazi I (637-658h),** AR Dirham | $50 |

1224

| 1224 | - Æ Dirham (SS 49) | $250 |
| 1225 | - Æ Fals | $25 |

		VF
1226	**Fakhr al-din Qara Arslan (658-693h)**, Æ Fals (SS 50)	$150
1227	**Najm al-din Ghazi II (693-712h)**, Æ Fals (SS 51)	$150
1228	**al-Salih Salih I (712-765h)**, AR Akçe	$50
1229	- Æ Double Fals (SS 53)	$1200
1230	- Æ Fals (SS 52)	$300
1231	- Æ Fals (SS 54)	*Extremely rare*
1232	- Æ Fals (SS 55)	$400
1233	**al-Mansur Ahmad (765-769h)**, AR Akçe	$75
1234	**al-Muzaffar Da'ud (769-778h)**, AR Akçe	$75
1235	- Æ Fals (SS 56)	$500
1236	**al-Zahir 'Isa (778-809h)**, AR Akçe	$75
1237	- Æ Fals (SS 57)	*Extremely rare*
1238	- Æ Fals (SS 58)	*Extremely rare*

ZENGID OF MOSUL

1239

1239	**Qutb al-din Mawdud (544-565h)**, AV Dinar	$600

1240

1240	- Æ Dirham (SS 59)	$150
1241	**Sayf al-din Ghazi II (565-576h)**, AV Dinar	$600

1242

1242	Æ Dirham (SS 60)	$200

1243

1243 - Æ Dirham (SS 61)

VF
$150

1244

1244 **'Izz al-din Mas'ud (576-589h),** AV Dinar

$400

1245

1245 - Æ Dirham (SS 62)

$250

1246

1246 - Æ Dirham (SS 63)
1247 **Nur al-din Arslanshah I (589-607h),** AV Dinar

$150
$300

1248

1248	- Æ Dirham (SS 64)	$300
1249	**'Izz al-din Mas'ud II (607-615h),** AV Dinar	$300

1250

1250	- Æ Dirham (SS 65)	$275
1251	**Nur al-din Arslanshah II (615-616h),** AV Dinar	$500

1252

1252	**Nasir al-din Mahmud (616-631h),** AV Dinar	$250

1253

1253	- Æ Dirham (SS 66)	$250

1254

1254   - Æ Dirham (SS 67) $150

LU'LU'ID

Jafar, Y., 'Dinars and History of Badr al-din Lu'lu' of Mosul', *JONS* 201, 2009

1255

1255   **Badr al-din Lu'lu' (631-657h),** AV Dinar $400

1256

1256   - AV Dinar, citing Möngke as overlord $600
1257   - BI Dirham (SS 69) $150

1258

1258   - Æ Dirham (SS 68) $150

1259

1259	- Æ Dirham (SS 71)	$150
1260	- Æ Fals (SS 70)	$150
1261	- Æ Fals, citing Möngke as overlord (SS 72)	$400
1262	**Rukn al-din Isma'il (657-660h),** AV Dinar	$600

1263

1263	- AV Dinar, citing Möngke as overlord	$800
1264	- AR Dirham	$300

ZENGID OF SYRIA

1265

1265	**Nur al-din Mahmud (541-569h),** Æ Fals (SS 73)	$150

1266

1266	- Æ Fals (SS 74)	$100

1267

1268

VF

1267	**al-Salih Isma'il (569-577h),** AR Dirham	$150
1268	- AR ½-Dirham	$100

1269

1269   - Æ Fals (SS 75) $50

1270

1271

1270	- Æ Fals (SS 76)	$125
1271	- Æ Fals (SS 77)	$50

ZENGID OF SINJAR

1272

1272   **'Imad al-din Zangi II (566-594h),** Æ Dirham (SS 78) $150

1273

		VF
1273	- Æ Dirham (SS 79)	$150
1274	**Qutb al-din Muhammad (594-616h),** Æ Dirham (SS 80)	$150

1275

1275	- Æ Dirham (SS 81)	$150

1276

1276	- Æ Dirham (SS 82)	$300
1277	- Æ Dirham (SS 83)	$250

1278

1278	**al-Amjad 'Umar (616-617h),** Æ Dirham (SS 84)	$500

ZENGID OF AL-JAZIRA

1279

		VF
1279	**Mu'izz al-din Sanjarshah (576-605h)**, Æ Dirham (SS 85)	$250
1280	- Æ Wuqiya (SS 86)	$275

1281

1281	**al-Mu'azzam Mahmud (605-648h)**, Æ Dirham (SS 87)	$250
1282	- Æ Dirham (SS 88)	$300

1283

1283	- Æ Dirham (SS 89)	$150

ZENGID OF SHAHRAZUR

1284	**'Imad al-din Zengi (fl.616-632h)**, AV Dinar	$500
1285	**Nur al-din Il-Arslan (fl.632-649h)**, AV Dinar	$600

BEGTEGINID

		1286	VF
1286	**Muzaffar al-din Kökburi (563-630h),** AV Dinar		$400
1287	- Æ Dirham, *obv.* seated figure		$300
1288	- Æ Dirham, *obv.* bust right		$250

1289

1289	- Æ Dirham, *obv.* lion-rider	$150

1290

1290	- Æ Fals, *obv.* seated figure, *rev.* hexagram	$250

BEGTIMURID

1291	**Sayf al-din Begtimur (579-589h),** Æ Fals, *obv.* cow	$250

SALDUQID

1292	**Diya' al-din Ghazi (fl.510-526h),** Æ Fals, *obv.* Virgin and Child	*Extremely rare*
1293	**Salduq b. 'Ali (523-563h),** Æ Fals, *obv.* two standing figures	$200
1294	**Muhammad b. Salduq (563-587h),** Æ Fals, *obv.* mounted archer	$250

MENKUJAKID

1295

		VF
1295	**Fakhr al-din Bakhramshah (c.563-622h)**, Æ Dirham, *obv.* Byzantine style half-length bust	$400
1296	- Æ Dirham, *obv.* head left within hexagon	$250
1297	- Æ Dirham, inscriptional type	$250
1298	**Sayf al-din Shahinshah (fl.573h)**, Æ Dirham	$600

DANISHMENDID

Whelan, E.J., 'A Contribution to Danishmendid History: The Figured Copper Coins', *ANS Museum Notes 25*, New York, 1980

1299	**Amir Ghazi (497-528h)**, Æ Dirham, *obv.* bust of Christ	*Extremely rare*

1300

1300	**Malik Muhammad (528-536h)**, Æ Dirham, Greek inscriptions	$800
1301	**'Ayn al-dawla Isma'il (536-547h)**, Æ Dirham, Greek inscriptions	$1000

1302

1302	**'Imad al-din Dhu'l-Nun (536-570h)**, Æ Dirham, *obv.* lion-rider	$650
1303	- Æ Dirham, bilingual type	$800
1304	- Æ Dirham, Arabic inscriptions only	$800

1305

		VF
1305	**Nizam al-din Yaghi Basan (537-559h),** Æ Dirham, *obv.* bust right	$500
1306	- Æ Dirham, Arabic inscriptions only	$750

1307

1307	**Dhu'l-Qarnayn (547-557h),** Æ Dirham, *obv.* bust right	$600

1308

1308	**Nasir al-din Muhammad (557-565h),** Æ Dirham, *obv.* two standing figures	$500
1309	- Æ Dirham, *obv.* horseman	$1200
1310	**Shams al-din Isma'il (559-567h),** Æ Dirham	$500
1311	**Fakhr al-din Qasim (565-567h),** Æ Dirham, *obv.* lion	$750

COUNTERMARKED BYZANTINE COINS

Lowick, N.M., Bendall, S., & Whitting, P.D., *The Mardin Hoard,* London, 1977

1312	Æ Follis, countermarked *atabeg*	$50
1313	Æ Follis, countermarked *'adl*	$50
1314	Æ Follis, countermarked *sa'd*	$125
1315	Æ Follis, countermarked *shams*	$50
1316	Æ Follis, countermarked *lillah*	$30
1317	Æ Follis, countermarked *najm*	$30

SELJUQ OF RUM

Broome, M., *A Survey of the Coinage of the Seljuqs of Rum*, London, 2011

1318

1318	**Mas'ud I (510-551h),** Æ Fals, *obv.* Byzantine bust	$600

1319

1319	**Qilij Arslan II (551-588h),** AR Dirham	$250
1320	- Æ Fals	$80
1321	**Kaykhusraw I, 1ˢᵗ reign (588-595h),** AR Dirham	$250
1322	- Æ Fals, *obv.* horseman	$50
1323	- Æ Fals, *obv.* facing bust	$250

1324

1324	**Tughril (c.588-618h),** AR Dinar	$200
1325	- Æ Fals	$125

1326   1327

1326	**Sulayman II (592-600h),** AR Dirham, horseman type	$1200
1327	- Æ Fals, *obv.* horseman	$75

1328

1328	**Kaykhusraw I, 2nd reign (600-607h),** AR Dirham	$300
1329	- Æ Fals	$50

1330

1330	**Kayka'us I (607-616h),** AR Dirham	$200
1331	- Æ Fals	$30

1332

1332	**Kayqubad I, as malik of Tokat (607-610h),** Æ Fals, *obv.* St George and the dragon	$600

1333

1333	**Kayqubad I (616-634h),** AV Dinar	$3000

1334 1335

		VF
1334	- AR Dirham	$80
1335	- AR Dirham, bilingual type (Armenia)	$600
1336	- Æ Fals	$30

1337

1337	**Kaykhusraw II (634-644h),** AV Dinar	$1500
1338	- AV Dinar, *obv.* sun and two lions	*Extremely rare*

1339 1340

1339	- AR Dirham	$40
1340	- AR Dirham, lion & sun type	$75

1341

1341	- AR Dirham, bilingual type (Armenia)	$400
1342	- Æ Fals	$30

1343

VF

1343   **Kayka'us II, 1st reign (643-647h)**, AV Dinar $1500

1344

1344   - AR Dirham $30
1345   - AR ½-Dirham $250
1346   - Æ Fals $30

1347

1347   **Qilij Arslan IV, 1st reign (646-647h)**, AR Dirham, horseman type $500

1348

1348   **Kayka'us II, Qilij Arslan IV, & Kayqubad II (647-657h)**, AV Dinar $1500

1349

1349   - AR Dirham $30

1350

1350	**Kayka'us II, 2nd reign (655-660h)**, AR Dirham	$40
1351	- Æ Fals	$150
1352	**Qilij Arslan IV, 2nd reign (655-664h)**, AV Dinar	$3000

1353

1353	- AR Dirham	$80
1354	- AR ½-Dirham	$300

1355

1355	**Kaykhusraw III (663-682h)**, AV Dinar	$3000

1356

1356	- AR Dirham	$40
1357	- AR ½-Dirham	$300
1358	- Æ Fals	$75

1359

		VF
1359	**Mas'ud II, 1st reign (679-697h)**, AR Dirham	$50
1360	- AR ½-Dirham	$500
1361	**Kayqubad III (697-701h)**, AR Dirham	$125
1362	- AR Dirham, lion & sun type	$250
1363	**Mas'ud II, 2nd reign (c.701-708h)**, AR Dirham	$250

BEYLIK OF KARESI

1364	**Beylerbeyi Çelebi (c.744-747h)**, AR Akçe	$200

BEYLIK OF SARUHAN

1365   1366

1365	**Ishaq b. Ilyas (c.759-792h)**, AR Akçe	$75
1366	- Æ Mangir	$100
1367	**Khisr b. Ishaq (792, 804-813h)**, AR Akçe	$125
1368	- Æ Mangir	$100
1369	**Urkhan (c.806-810h)**, Æ Mangir	$200
1370	**Anonymous,** Æ Mangir	$75

BEYLIK OF MENTESHE

1371	**Ahmad Ghazi (759-793h)**, AR Akçe	$75

1372

1372	**Ilyas b. Muhammad, 2nd reign (805-823h)**, AR Akçe	$40

BEYLIK OF AYDIN

		VF
1373	**'Isa Beg (c.762-789h),** AR Akçe	$40
1374	**Mehmed b. Umur (fl.807h),** AR Akçe	$150
1375	- Æ Mangir	$150
1376	**Junayd b. Ibrahim (813-816, 825-829h),** AR Akçe	$150
1377	- Æ Mangir	$150
1378	**Mustafa Beg (824-825h),** AR Akçe	$200
1379	**Anonymous,** Æ Mangir	$75

BEYLIK OF GERMIYAN

1380	**Muhammad Beg (741-762h),** AR Akçe	$150
1381	**Sulaymanshah (762-789h),** AR Akçe	$150
1382	**Ya'qub b. Sulayman (789-792, 805-832h),** AR Akçe	$150
1383	**Anonymous,** AR Akçe	$100
1384	- AR Akçe, citing Timur	$150

HAMIDID

1385	**Anonymous,** AR Dirham	$100
1386	**Jalis Bey (fl.758h),** Æ Fals	$100

BEYLIK OF ALANYA

1387	**Anonymous,** AR Dirham	$100
1388	- AR Akçe	$40

1389

1389	**Saveji b. Shams al-din (fl.827h),** AR Akçe	$100
1390	**Qaraman b. Saveji (fl.827-834h),** AR Akçe	$100

KARAMANID

1391	**Anonymous,** AR Dirham	$80
1392	**Badr b. Qaraman (c.717-731h),** AR Dirham, countermarked type	$125
1393	**'Ala al-din (762-800h),** AR Dirham	$150

1394   VF

1394	Muhammad b. 'Ala al-din (805-822, 824-827h), AR Dirham	$100
1395	'Ali b. 'Ala al-din (822-824h), AR Dirham	$200
1396	Ibrahim (824, 827-868h), AR Dirham	$125

1397

1397	- AR Akçe	$75
1398	Ishaq b. Ibrahim (868-869h), AR Akçe	$150
1399	Pir Ahmad (869-871h), AR Akçe	$150

ISFENDIYARID

| 1400 | *temp.* Sulayman (709-742h), AR Akçe | $100 |
| 1401 | *temp.* 'Adil Beg (c.746-760h), AR ½-Akçe | $50 |

1402

1402	Koturum Bayezit (762-787h), AR Akçe	$40
1403	- AR ½-Akçe	$100
1404	Suleyman II (787-794h), AR Akçe	$40
1405	Isfendiyar (794-843h), AV ½-Ashrafi	*Extremely rare*
1406	- AR Akçe	$30
1407	- Æ Mangir	$100

ERETNID

1408

1408	*temp.* Eretna (736-753h), AR Akçe	$40
1409	Muhammad b. Eretna (753-767h), AR Akçe	$60
1410	'Ala al-din (c.756-759h), AR Akçe	$150
1411	Muzaffar al-din (c.757-760h), AR Akçe	$100

1412

1412	**'Ali Beg (767-782h),** AR Akçe	$50
1413	- AR ½-Akçe	$200

QADIS OF SIVAS

1414	**Burhan al-din Ahmad (782-800h),** AR Akçe	$150

PRE-MONGOL IRAN, AFGHANISTAN, & CENTRAL ASIA

As the power of the Abbasid caliphate declined in the late 3rd and early 4th centuries AH, many autonomous dynasties were established throughout Iran, Afghanistan, and Central Asia, and this process only intensified after the fall of Baghdad to the Buwayhids in 334h. The most important of the post-Abbasid dynasties were the Buwayhids in Iran, the Samanids in Khurasan and Central Asia, the Ghaznavids in Khurasan and Afghanistan, and the Qarakhanids in Central Asia. The 5th century AH saw the arrival of the Seljuqs and their conquest of Iran and the Jazira. However, the Seljuq hegemony lasted only a few decades before their kingdom split into numerous smaller states; many of these were vassal states of the Seljuqs in theory but independent in practice. In the early 7th century AH the Mongol invasions began, and in less than fifty years the Mongols had conquered all of the Eastern Islamic world.

TAHIRID

1415

			VF
1415	**Tahir b. al-Husayn (205-207h),** AR Dirham (common mint: Herat)		$125

1416

1416	- Æ Fals	$250

1417

1417	**Talha b. Tahir (207-213h),** AR Dirham (common mint: Samarqand)	$75

1418

		VF
1418	- Æ Fals	$250
1419	- Æ Fals, *rev.* Sasanian bust	$300
1420	**'Abd Allah b. Tahir (213-230h),** Æ Fals	$300

1421

1421	**Tahir b. 'Abd Allah (230-248h),** Æ Fals	$80
1422	**Muhammad b. Tahir (248-259h),** Æ Fals	$150

ZANJ REBELLION

1423	**'Ali b. Muhammad (258-271h),** AV Dinar	*Extremely rare*

1424

1424	- AR Dirham	$2500

DULAFID

1425

1425	**Ahmad b. 'Abd al-'Aziz (265-280h),** AV Dinar	$2500
1426	- AV Dinar, donative type	*Extremely rare*
1427	- AR Dirham	$200

VF

| 1428 | **'Umar b. 'Abd al-'Aziz (280-284h),** AV Dinar | $2000 |

1429

| 1429 | - AR Dirham | $250 |

KHUJISTANID

1430

| 1430 | **Ahmad b. 'Abd Allah (fl.261-268h),** AR Dirham
(common mint: Nishapur) | $100 |

HARTHAMID

| 1431 | **Rafi' b. Harthama (268-283h),** AV Dinar | *Extremely rare* |
| 1432 | - AR Dirham | $1000 |

SAFFARID

Lloyd, S., 'The coinage of the Saffarids of Sijistan and related dynasties, 247h-332h', Parts 1 & 2, *JONS* 219-220, 2014 (further parts forthcoming)
Walker, J., *The Coinage of the second Saffarid dynasty in Sistan,* ANS Numismatic Notes and Monographs No. 72, New York, 1936

| 1433 | **Ya'qub b. al-Layth (247-265h),** AV Dinar | *Extremely rare* |

1434

| 1434 | - AR Dirham | $150 |

1435

		VF
1435	- AR Dirham, donative type	*Extremely rare*
1436	- Æ Fals	$750
1437	**Anonymous,** BI Drachm, bull & horseman type	$50
1438	**'Amr b. al-Layth (265-288h),** AV Dinar	*Extremely rare*

1439

1439	- AR double Dirham	$600

1440

1440	- AR Dirham (common mints: Shiraz, Fars)	$75
1441	- AR Dirham, donative type	*Extremely rare*[1]

1442

1442	**Mansur b. Shurkub, rebel (fl.269h),** AR Dirham	$200

1443

1443   **Muhammad b. 'Amr, viceroy (272-274h)**, AR Dirham $125
         (common mints: Shiraz, Fars)

1444

1444   **Tahir b. Muhammad (288-296h)**, AR Dirham $75
         (common mint: Fars)

1445

1445   **al-Layth b. 'Ali (296-298h)**, AR Dirham $150
1446   **Subkari, rebel (296-298h)**, AR Dirham $150
1447   **al-Mu'addal b. 'Ali (298-299h)**, AR Dirham $750
1448   **Muhammad b. Hurmuz (299-300h)**, AR Dirham   *Extremely rare*

1449

1449   **Kuthayyir b. Ahmad (c.305-306h)**, AR Dirham $300
1450   **Ahmad b. Qudam (c.307-310h)**, AV Dinar   *Extremely rare*

1451

1451	- AR Dirham	$300
1452	**'Abd Allah b. Ahmad (310-311h)**, AR Dirham	$750
1453	**Ahmad b. Muhammad (311-352h)**, AV Dinar	$1500

1454

1455

1454	- AV fractional Dinar	$250
1455	- AR Dirham	$200
1456	- Æ Fals	$50
1457	**Khalaf b. Ahmad, 1ˢᵗ reign (352-353h)**, AV fractional Dinar	$150
1458	**Tahir b. Muhammad (353-359h)**, AV fractional Dinar	$250
1459	**al-Husayn b. Tahir, 1ˢᵗ & 2ⁿᵈ reigns (359-361h)**, AV fractional Dinar	$150

1460

1461

1460	**Khalaf b. Ahmad, 2ⁿᵈ reign (360-369h)**, AV fractional Dinar	$150
1461	- Æ Fals	$75

1462

1462	**al-Husayn b. Tahir, 3ʳᵈ reign (c.369-371h)**, AV fractional Dinar	$150
1463	- AV fractional Dinar, citing Nuh b. Mansur	$300

1464

		VF
1464	**Khalaf b. Ahmad, 3rd reign (370-393h),** AV fractional Dinar	$200
1465	- AR Dirham	$300
1466	- Æ Fals	$100
1467	**'Amr b. Khalaf (d.383h),** AV fractional Dinar	$500
1468	**Tahir b. Khalaf (fl.391-392h),** AV fractional Dinar	$400

1469

1469	- AR Dirham	$200
1470	**Nasr b. Ahmad (c.442-465h),** AV Dinar	*Extremely rare*

1471

1471	**Taj al-din Harb (564-610h),** BI Jital	$25
1472	**Taj al-din Nasr (618h),** BI Jital	$50

1473

1473	**Abu Mansur (618-619h),** BI Jital	$50

BANIJURID

1474	**Da'ud b. Muhammad (fl.260h),** AR Dirham	$400
1475	**Muhammad b. Ahmad (260-285h),** AR Dirham	$75
1476	**Sa'id b. Shu'ayb (c.266-274h),** AR Dirham	$100
1477	**Muhammad b. 'Umar (fl.268h),** AR Dirham	$400

1478

		VF
1478	**Ahmad b. Muhammad (c.285-297h),** AR Dirham	$75
1479	**Ahmad b. Muhammad b. Yahya (c.295-297h),** AR Dirham	$200
1480	**Ja'far b. Ahmad (c.310-313h),** AR Dirham	$500

AMIRS OF AL-KHUTTAL

1481

1481	**al-Harith b. Asad (c.280-293h),** AR Dirham	$300
1482	**al-Harith b. Mansur (c.420-437h),** AR Dirham	*Extremely rare*

SAMANID

1483

1483	**Nuh b. Asad (204-227h),** Æ Fals	$125
1484	**Ahmad b. Asad (204-250h),** Æ Fals	$80

1485

1485	**Yahya b. Asad (204-241h),** Æ Fals	$150

1486   **VF**

1486	**Nasr I b. Ahmad (250-279h),** Æ Fals	$60
1487	**Ya'qub b. Ahmad (fl.265h),** Æ Fals	$100
1488	**Nuh II b. Asad (fl.274-279h),** Æ Fals	$150

1489

1489   **Isma'il b. Ahmad (279-295h),** AV Dinar $500

1490

1490   - AR Dirham (common mints: Samarqand, al-Shash) $40

1491

1491   - Æ Fals $40

1492

1492   **Ahmad b. Isma'il (295-301h),** AV Dinar $500

1493

| 1493 | - AR Dirham (common mints: Andaraba, al-Shash) | $50 |
| 1494 | **Ishaq b. Ahmad (301h),** AV Dinar | *Extremely rare* |

1495

| 1495 | - AR Dirham | $600 |
| 1496 | - Æ Fals | $300 |

1497   1498

1497	**Nasr II b. Ahmad (301-331h),** AV Dinar (common mints: al-Muhammadiya, Nishapur)	$250
1498	- AV Dinar, donative type	$4000
1499	- AR multiple Dirham, struck posthumously	$150

1500

| 1500 | - AR Dirham (common mints: Balkh, Samarqand, al-Shash) | $40 |

1501

VF

1501   - AR Dirham, donative type

$600

1502

1502   - Æ Fals $30
1503   **Ahmad b. Sahl, rebel (fl.301-308h),** AV Dinar $1500

1504

1504   - AR Dirham (common mint: Andaraba) $80
1505   **Layla b. Nu'man (fl.309h),** AR Dirham $1000
1506   **Yahya b. Ahmad, rebel (c.315-319h),** AV Dinar $2500

1507

1507   - AR Dirham $800

1508

VF

| 1508 | **Nuh b. Nasr (331-343h),** AV Dinar (common mint: Nishapur) | $250 |
| 1509 | - AR multiple Dirham | $60 |

1510

| 1510 | - AR Dirham (common mint: Samarqand) | $40 |
| 1511 | - Æ Fals | $60 |

1512

| 1512 | **Ibrahim b. Ahmad, rebel (335h),** AV Dinar | $1500 |
| 1513 | - AR Dirham | *Extremely rare* |

1514

| 1514 | **'Abd al-Malik b. Nuh (343-350h),** AV Dinar (common mint: Nishapur) | $400 |

1515

| 1515 | - AR Dirham | $60 |
| 1516 | - Æ Fals | $100 |

1517

1517	**Mansur I b. Nuh (350-365h),** AV Dinar	$400
1518	- AR multiple Dirham	$100

1519

1519	- AR Dirham	$75

1520

1520	- AE Fals	$20

1521

1521	**Nuh b. Mansur (365-387h),** AV Dinar (common mint: Nishapur)	$300
1522	- AR multiple Dirham	$80

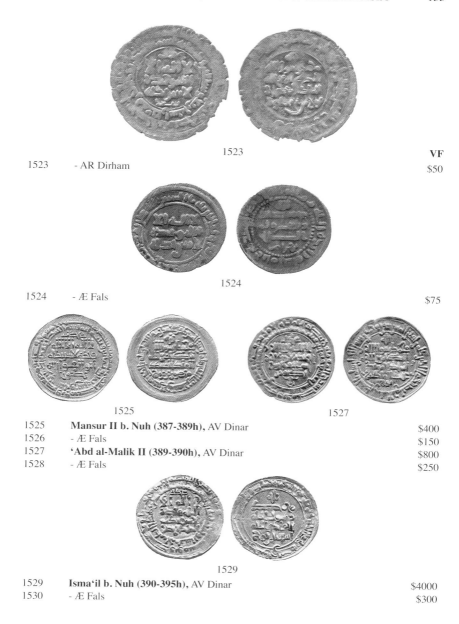

1523

VF

| 1523 | - AR Dirham | $50 |

1524

| 1524 | - Æ Fals | $75 |

1525   1527

1525	**Mansur II b. Nuh (387-389h),** AV Dinar	$400
1526	- Æ Fals	$150
1527	**'Abd al-Malik II (389-390h),** AV Dinar	$800
1528	- Æ Fals	$250

1529

| 1529 | **Isma'il b. Nuh (390-395h),** AV Dinar | $4000 |
| 1530 | - Æ Fals | $300 |

SAMANID OF AKHSIKATH

1531

		VF
1531	**Asad b. Ahmad (c.250-270h),** Æ Fals	$100
1532	**Ahmad b. Asad (c.270-277h),** Æ Fals	$150

1533

1533	**Ishaq b. Ahmad (c.277-290h),** Æ Fals	$125
1534	**Muhammad b. Asad (fl.303h),** Æ Fals	$250

1535

1535	**Malik b. Shakartegin (fl.312-334h),** Æ Fals	$75

1536

1536	**Bakr b. Malik (fl.335-341h),** Æ Fals	$125

AFSHINID

1537	**Siyar b. 'Abd Allah (fl.279-280h),** Æ Fals	$300

MUHTAJID

		VF
1538	**Nasr b. Ahmad (fl.341-365h)**, Æ Fals	$125

AMIRS OF BUST

1539	**Khut-tegin I (fl.337-341h)**, Æ Fals	$200
1540	**Muhammad b. Khut-tegin (fl.347-348h)**, Æ Fals	$150
1541	**Bekchur (fl.349-350h)**, Æ Fals	$200
1542	**Baytuz (fl.359-365h)**, Æ Fals	$200
1543	**Takantash (fl.367-369h)**, Æ Fals	$250

AFRIGHID

1544

| 1544 | **Ahmad b. Muhammad (c.348-366h)**, Æ Fals | $200 |

KHAZARS

| 1545 | **Anonymous,** AR Dirham, imitating Abbasid prototypes | $400 |
| 1546 | - AR Dirham, imitating Samanid prototypes | $750 |

VOLGA BULGARS

| 1547 | **Talib b. Ahmad (338-347h)**, AR Dirham | $1500 |

1548

| 1548 | **Mika'il b. Ja'far (c.350h)**, AR Dirham | $750 |
| 1549 | **Anonymous,** AR Dirham, imitating Samanid prototypes | $300 |

AMIRS OF ANDARABA

1550   **Harb b. Sahlan (c.344-365h),** AR Dirham $150

1551

1551   **Maktum (fl.347-364h),** AR Dirham $250

1552

1552   **Sahlan b. Maktum (fl.364-378h),** AR multiple Dirham $125

1553   - AR Dirham $250

1554

1554   **al-Harith b. Harb,** AR multiple Dirham $125

AMIR OF WARWARLIZ

1555   **'Ali (fl.374h),** AR multiple Dirham $250

SAJID

1556

1556	**al-Afshin b. Diwdad (276-288h),** AR Dirham	$500
1557	- AR Dirham, donative type	*Extremely rare*
1558	**Yusuf b. Diwdad (288-315h),** AV Dinar	$1200

1559

1559	- AR Dirham	$400
1560	- AR Dirham, donative type	*Extremely rare*

1561

1561   **al-Fath b. al-Afshin (315-317h),** AV Dinar $1500

1562

1562	- AR Dirham	$500
1563	**Muflih al-Yusufi (c.317-323h),** AV Dinar	$1200
1564	- AR Dirham	*Extremely rare*

KURDS OF ADHARBAYJAN

VF

1565	**Daysam b. Ibrahim (c.325-341h),** AV Dinar	$2500
1566	- AR Dirham	$800

SHADDADID

1567

1567	**al-Fadl b. Muhammad (375-422h),** AR Dirham	$30

1568

1568	**Shawur b. al-Fadl (441-459h),** AR Dirham	$250

SU'LUKID

Miles, G.C., *The Numismatic History of Rayy,* ANS Numismatic Studies No. 2, New York, 1938

1569	**Muhammad b. 'Ali, 1ˢᵗ reign (c.301-302h),** AV Dinar	*Extremely rare*
1570	- AR Dirham	*Extremely rare*

1571

1571	**Ahmad b. 'Ali (fl.304-311h),** AV Dinar	$500

1572

1572   - AR Dirham $250

1573

1573   **Muhammad b. 'Ali, 2nd reign (c.314-316h),** AV Dinar $400

1574

1574   - AR Dirham $250

BUWAYHID

Treadwell, L., *Buyid Coinage,* Oxford, 2001

1575

1575   **'Imad al-dawla 'Ali b. Buwayh, as 'Ali b. Buwayh (322-334h),** $40
            AR Dirham (common mint: Shiraz)

1576   1577   **VF**

| 1576 | **- as 'Imad al-dawla (334-338h),** AV Dinar | $500 |
| 1577 | - - AR Dirham | $50 |

1578

| 1578 | **Mu'izz al-dawla Ahmad b. Buwayh, as Ahmad b. Buwayh (328-334h),** AR Dirham | $125 |

1579

| 1579 | **- as Mu'izz al-dawla (334-356h),** AV Dinar (common mint: Madinat al-Salam) | $500 |

1580

| 1580 | - - AR Dirham (common mints: al-Basra, Madinat al-Salam) | $50 |
| 1581 | **Rukn al-dawla al-Hasan b. Buwayh, as al-Hasan b. Buwayh, governor of Khuzistan (c.328-331h),** AR Dirham | *Extremely rare* |

1582

1582   **- as Rukn al-dawla (335-366h),** AV Dinar $500

1583

1583   - - AR Dirham $50
1584   **'Adud al-dawla Abu Shuja', as Abu Shuja' (338-341h),** AV Dinar $600
1585   - AR Dirham (common mints: Arrajan, Siraf) $75

1586

1586   **- as 'Adud al-dawla (341-372h),** AV Dinar (common mint: al-Basra) $300

1587

1587   - - AR Dirham (common mints: Arrajan, Shiraz) $40

1588

1588   - - AR Dirham, hexagonal design on both sides $150

VF

1589	**Mu'ayyid al-dawla Abu Mansur (356-373h)**, AV Dinar	$500
1590	- AR Dirham (common mint: Isbahan)	$50

1591

1591	**'Izz al-dawla Bakhtiyar (356-367h)**, AV Dinar	$600

1592

1592	- AR Dirham	$80
1593	**Sanad al-dawla Abu Harb (fl.357h)**, AR Dirham	*Extremely rare*

1594

1594	**Fakhr al-dawla 'Ali b. Rukn al-dawla, as 'Ali b. Rukn al-dawla, governor in Hamadan (359-364h)**, AR Dirham	$125
1595	- as Fakhr al-dawla, governor in Hamadan (365-369h), AV Dinar	$600
1596	- - AR Dirham	$80
1597	- as Fakhr al-dawla, independent ruler (373-387h), AV Dinar	$500

1598

1598	- - AR Dirham	$50

1599   **VF**

| 1599 | **Sharaf al-dawla Abu'l-Fawaris Shirdhil, as Shirdhil, governor of Kirman (c.361-372h),** AR Dirham | $100 |
| 1600 | **- as Abu'l-Fawaris (c.370-377h),** AV Dinar | *Extremely rare* |

1601

1601	- - AR Dirham	$75
1602	**- as Sharaf al-dawla (c.377-379h),** AV Dinar	*Extremely rare*
1603	- - AR Dirham	$150

1604

1604	**Samsam al-dawla al-Marzuban, as al-Marzuban (362-372h),** AV Dinar (common mint: Suq al-Ahwaz)	$400
1605	- AR Dirham	$50
1606	**- as Samsam al-dawla (372-376h, 380-388h),** AV Dinar	$1500

1607

| 1607 | - - AR Dirham (common mint: Shiraz) | $50 |
| 1608 | **Diya' al-dawla b. 'Adud al-dawla (fl.372h),** AR Dirham | *Extremely rare* |

1609

VF

1609   **Abu'l-Husayn Ahmad (372-375h),** AV Dinar $400

1610

1610   - AR Dirham $50
1611   **Khusrafiruz b. Rukn al-dawla (373-384h),** AV Dinar   *Extremely rare*

1612

1612   - AR Dirham $125

1613

1613   **Baha' al-dawla Abu Nasr (379-403h),** AV Dinar, fine gold $250
          (common mint: Suq al-Ahwaz)
1614   - AV Dinar, base gold $125

1615

1615   - AR Dirham $60

VF

1616	**Majd al-dawla Abu Talib, as Abu Talib (387-389h)**, AR Dirham	$40
1617	**- as Majd al-dawla (389-420h)**, AV Dinar	$1200
1618	- - AR Dirham	$50
1619	**Shams al-dawla Abu Tahir (387-412h)**, AV Dinar	*Extremely rare*
1620	- AR Dirham	$125
1621	**Sultan al-dawla Abu Shuja' (403-415h)**, AV Dinar	$800

1622

1622	- AR Dirham	$150
1623	- AR ½-Dirham	*Extremely rare*
1624	**Qawam al-dawla Abu'l-Fawaris, as Abu'l-Fawaris (fl.407h)**, AR Dirham	$200

1625

| 1625 | **- as Qawam al-dawla (fl.416h)**, AR Dirham | $250 |

1626

| 1626 | **Abu Kalijar b. Sultan al-dawla (415-440h)**, AV Dinar (common mint: Suq al-Ahwaz) | $275 |

1627

1627	- AR Dirham	$300
1628	- AR donative fractional Dirham	*Extremely rare*
1629	**Abu Kalijar b. Majd al-dawla (fl.432h)**, AV Dinar	*Extremely rare*
1630	**Jalal al-dawla Abu Tahir (fl.435h)**, AR Dirham	$1200
1631	**Abu Mansur Fulad Sutun (fl.440h)**, AR Dirham	*Extremely rare*

1632

1632	**Abu Nasr Khusrafiruz (440-447h)**, AV Dinar	$400
1633	- AR Dirham	$400

SALLARID

1634	**al-Marzuban b. Muhammad (330-346h)**, AV Dinar	$3000
1635	- AR Dirham	$400
1636	**Wahsudan b. Muhammad (c.330-357h)**, AR Dirham	$250
1637	**Justan b. al-Marzuban (c.346-349h)**, AV Dinar	$4000
1638	- AR Dirham	$400
1639	**Ibrahim b. al-Marzuban (c.349-355h)**, AV Dinar	*Extremely rare*
1640	- AR Dirham	$500
1641	**Isma'il b. Wahsudan (fl.350-355h)**, AR Dirham	$600
1642	**Nuh b. Wahsudan (fl.355h)**, AR Dirham	$600
1643	**Sharmazan b. Mishaki (fl.355-361h)**, AR Dirham	*Extremely rare*
1644	**Rustam b. Justan (fl.359-362h)**, AR Dirham	$600

ZAYDI IMAMS OF HAWSAM

1645	**Ja'far b. Muhammad al-Tha'ir (c.319-350h)**, AR Dirham	$750

JASTANID

			VF
1646	**Manadhir b. Jastan (c.336-361h),** AV Dinar		$4000
1647	- AV fractional Dinar		$1500

1648

1648	**Khusrashah b. Manadhir (fl.361-368h),** AR Dirham	$250

JULANDID

1649	**Badr b. Khattal (fl.334h),** AR Dirham	$1000
1650	**al-'Abbas b. Ja'far (fl.336h),** AR Dirham	$1000

1651

1651	**Ridwan b. Ja'far (fl.338-349h),** AR Dirham	$300

HASANWAYHID

1652   1653

1652	**Badr b. Hasanwayh (369-405h),** AV Dinar	$1200
1653	- AR Dirham	$150

KAKWAYHID

1654

1654	**Muhammad b. Dushmanzar (398-433h)**, AV Dinar	$500

1655

1655	- AR Dirham	$250

1656

1656	**Faramurz (433-443h)**, AV Dinar	$250

'ANNAZID

1657	**Husam al-dawla Faris (401-437h)**, AR Dirham	$750
1658	**'Ali b. 'Umar (fl.417h)**, AR Dirham	$400

'ALID

1659

1659	**Anonymous**, AR Dirham	$150
1660	**al-Hasan b. Zayd (250-270h)**, AV Dinar	*Extremely rare*

1661

		VF
1661	- AR Dirham	$250
1662	**al-Husayn b. Ahmad (fl.250-253h),** AR Dirham	$1000
1663	**Ahmad b. Muhammad (fl.270h),** AR Dirham	*Extremely rare*[2]
1664	**Muhammad b. Zayd (270-287h),** AV Dinar	*Extremely rare*
1665	- AR Dirham	*Extremely rare*
1666	**al-Hasan b. al-Qasim, 1ˢᵗ reign (306-311h),** AV Dinar	$3000
1667	**Ja'far b. al-Hasan (311-314h),** AV Dinar	*Extremely rare*

1668

1668   *temp.* **al-Hasan b. al-Qasim, 2ⁿᵈ reign (314-316h),** AV Dinar $500

ZIYARID

1669

1669	**Mardawij b. Ziyar (315-323h),** AV Dinar (common mint: Mah al-Basra)	$400
1670	- AR Dirham	*Extremely rare*
1671	**Bakran b. Khurshid (fl.323h),** AV Dinar	$3000

1672

1672   **Bisutun b. Wushmagir (357-367h)**, AV Dinar $2500

1673

1673   - AR Dirham, in his own name $250

1674

1674   - AR Dirham, in the name of his father $125

1675   1676

1675   **Qabus b. Wushmagir (367-403h)**, AV Dinar $2500
1676   - AR Dirham $250

1677

1677	- BI Dirham		**VF** $250

1678

1678	**Falak al-Ma'ali Manuchihr (403-420h)**, BI Dirham	$250
1679	**Sharaf al-Ma'ali Anushirvan (420-441h)**, AV Dinar	*Extremely rare[3]*

ZIYARID OF THE JIBAL

1680	**Farhad b. Mardawij (fl.415-425h)**, AR Dirham	$500

FIRUZANID

1681

1681	**al-Hasan b. al-Firuzan (330-356h)**, AV Dinar	$2500

BAVANDID

1682	**Rustam b. Sharwin (c.352-370h)**, AV Dinar	*Extremely rare*

³   Baldwin's Islamic Coin Auction 13, 30 October 2007, lot 361

1683

		VF
1683	- AR Dirham	$300
1684	**Shahriyar b. Rustam (fl.377-393h)**, AR Dirham	$600
1685	**Shahriyar b. Qarin (466-504h)**, AV Dinar	$300
1686	**Wishtahm b. Qarin (fl.510h)**, AV Dinar	*Extremely rare*
1687	**'Ali b. Shahriyar (511-534h)**, AV Dinar	$400
1688	**Rustam b. 'Ali (c.534-557h)**, AV Dinar	$600
1689	**al-Hasan b. Rustam (c.557-567h)**, AV Dinar	$600

'IMRANID

1690

1690	**Muhadhdhab al-dawla (376-408h)**, AR Dirham	$300

RAWWADID

1691	**Muhammad b. Husayn (c.378-407h)**, AR Dirham	$500

HADHABANI KURDS

1692	**Abu'l-Hayja b. Rabib al-dawla (fl.425h)**, BI Dirham	$200
1693	**Jastan b. Rabib al-dawla (fl.451-452h)**, BI Dirham	$250

AMIRS OF YUN

1694	**Muhammad II Pakh (fl.424-432h)**, AR Dirham	$600

GHAZNAVID

		VF
1695	**Ibrahim b. 'Abd al-Ghaffar (c.338-345h),** Æ Fals	$125

1696

| 1696 | **Sebuktekin (366-387h),** AV Dinar | $400 |

1697   1698

1697	- AR Dirham, broad flan	$125
1698	- AR Dirham, small flan	$40
1699	**Isma'il (387-388h),** AR Dirham	$75

1700

| 1700 | **Mahmud, as Samanid governor (384-389h),** AV Dinar (common mint: Nishapur) | $400 |
| 1701 | - AR multiple Dirham | $125 |

1702

| 1702 | - AR Dirham | $60 |

1703

1703	**Mahmud (389-421h),** AV Dinar (common mints: Ghazna, Nishapur, Herat)	$275
1704	- AR multiple Dirham	$75
1705	- AR Dirham, broad flan	$75

1706

| 1706 | - AR Dirham, small flan | $25 |

1707

1707	- AR Dirham, bilingual type	$125
1708	- Æ Fals, large flan	$150
1709	**Nasr b. Sebuktekin, governor in Sijistan (c.400-412h),** AR Dirham	$200
1710	**Muhammad, as governor in Juzjan (fl.414h),** AR Dirham	$125
1711	**Muhammad, 1ˢᵗ reign (421h),** AV Dinar	$500
1712	- AR Dirham	$200
1713	- Æ Fals	$300

1714

| 1714 | **Mas'ud I (421-432h),** AV Dinar (common mints: Ghazna, Nishapur) | $300 |
| 1715 | - AR double Dirham | $125 |

1716

1716	- AR Dirham	$40
1717	- BI Dirham, bull & horseman type	$60

1718   1720

1718	**Mawdud (432-440h),** AV Dinar	$400
1719	- AR Dirham	$50
1720	- BI Jital	$25

1721

1721	**'Abd al-Rashid (440-443h),** AV Dinar	$500
1722	- AR Dirham	$60
1723	- BI Jital	$40

1724

1724	**Tughril (443-444h),** AV Dinar	$800
1725	- AR Dirham	$250
1726	**Farrukhzad (444-451h),** AV Dinar	$400
1727	- AR Dirham	$40
1728	- BI Jital	$25
1729	**Ibrahim (451-492h),** AV Dinar	$250
1730	- AR Dirham	$25

1731

1731	- BI Jital	$25
1732	**Mas'ud III (492-508h)**, AV Dinar	$400
1733	- AR Dirham	$40
1734	- BI Jital	$25
1735	**Malik Arslan (509-511h)**, BI Jital	$40
1736	**Bahramshah (511-552h)**, AV Dinar	$300
1737	- AR Dirham	$25
1738	- BI Jital	$25
1739	**Khusrawshah (552-555h)**, AV Dinar	$400
1740	- AR Dirham	$40
1741	- BI Jital	$40
1742	**Khusraw Malik (555-582h)**, AR Dirham	$75

1743

1743	- BI Jital	$25

PROTO-QARAKHANID

1744	**Malik Aram Yinal Qaraj**, Æ Cash	$400

QARAKHANID

Fedorov, M., 'The Qysmychi Hoard of Qarakhanid Dirhams (1002-1021)', *Numismatic Chronicle*, 2000

1745

1745	**Nasr b. 'Ali (c.383-403h)**, AV Dinar	$600

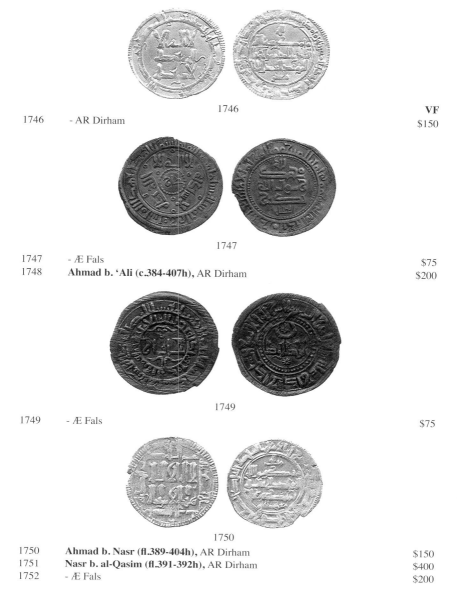

1746

VF

1746   - AR Dirham $150

1747

1747   - Æ Fals $75
1748   **Ahmad b. 'Ali (c.384-407h),** AR Dirham $200

1749

1749   - Æ Fals $75

1750

1750   **Ahmad b. Nasr (fl.389-404h),** AR Dirham $150
1751   **Nasr b. al-Qasim (fl.391-392h),** AR Dirham $400
1752   - Æ Fals $200

1753

1753   **Muhammad b. 'Ali (c.393-415h)**, AR Dirham $150

1754

1754   - Æ Fals $75
1755   **Bakr b. al-Hasan (fl.393-400h)**, Æ Fals $150
1756   **Yusuf b. 'Abd Allah, 1ˢᵗ reign (394-396h)**, Æ Fals $75

1757

1757   - Æ Fals, lion on obverse $150
1758   **Yusuf b. Harun (c.395-423h)**, AR Dirham $200
1759   - AR fractional Dirham $300
1760   - Æ Fals $200

1761

1761   **Nizam al-dawla (fl.399-404h)**, AR Dirham $150

1762

1762   - Æ Fals $125

1763

1763	**Yusuf b. 'Abd Allah, 2ⁿᵈ reign (403-405h)**, Æ Fals	$100
1764	**Mansur b. 'Ali (403-415h)**, AR Dirham	$150
1765	**al-Husayn b. al-Hasan (fl.404-418h)**, AR Dirham	$250
1766	- Æ Fals	$150
1767	**al-Husayn b. Mansur (fl.406-407h)**, AR Dirham	$250

1768

1768	- Æ Fals	$125
1769	**'Imad al-dawla Chaghri-Tegin (fl.407-417h)**, AR Dirham	$300

1770

1770	**Ibrahim b. Nasr, as governor (c.408-431h)**, Æ Fals	$125
1771	**'Abd al-Rahman b. Mansur (fl.409h)**, Æ Fals	$200
1772	**Ahmad b. Muhammad (fl.411h)**, Æ Fals	$150
1773	**'Ali b. Nasr (fl.411h)**, Æ Fals	$250

1774

		VF
1774	**'Ali b. al-Hasan (411-426h)**, AR Dirham	$250
1775	- Æ Fals	$150
1776	**Ahmad b. al-Hasan (fl.413-414h)**, Æ Fals	$200
1777	**al-'Abbas b. Muhammad (fl.415-433h)**, AR Dirham	$250
1778	**Kujtegin (fl.416-425h)**, AR Dirham	$150
1779	- Æ Fals	$200
1780	**Yusuf b. 'Ali (416-433h)**, Æ Fals	$150
1781	**Sulayman b. Harun (fl.416-426h)**, Æ Fals	$150
1782	**Muhammad b. Yusuf (421-449h)**, AR Dirham	$250
1783	- BI Dirham	$200
1784	**Rukn al-dawla (fl.421-423h)**, Æ Fals	$250
1785	**Muhammad b. al-Hasan, 2nd reign (428-433h)**, AR Dirham	$300

1786

1786	**Ibrahim b. Nasr (431-460h)**, Æ Fals	$100
1787	**Rukn al-din Mas'ud (556-566h)**, AV Dinar	$750
1788	- Æ Dirham	$60

1789

1789	**Ibrahim b. al-Husayn, at Uzkand (551-574h)**, Æ Dirham	$125
1790	**Nasr b. al-Husayn (fl.564-568h)**, Æ Dirham	$150
1791	**Muhammad b. Mas'ud (566-574h)**, Æ Dirham	$100
1792	**Malik Yaghan Khan (c.573-574h)**, Æ Dirham	$200
1793	**Ibrahim b. al-Husayn, as Khan (574-599h)**, AV Dinar	$600
1794	**Jalal al-din Muhammad (fl.574-598h)**, Æ Dirham	$300

		VF
1795	**Khusrawshah (c.576-583h)**, Æ Dirham	$200
1796	**Tughril Khaqan (fl.586-591h)**, Æ Dirham, small flan	$250
1797	**'Imad al-din Ulugh Akdash (fl.596-602h)**, Æ Dirham	$150

1798

| 1798 | **Sulayman Tafghaj Khan**, Æ Dirham | $75 |

QARAKHANID VASSALS

| 1799 | **Mansur b. Ahmad (fl.382-389h)**, Æ Fals | $100 |
| 1800 | **Muhammad b. Mansur (fl.391-395h)**, Æ Fals | $75 |

1801

1801	**Muzaffar Kiya (fl.395-406h)**, AR Dirham	$150
1802	**Salar b. Muhammad (fl.399h)**, Æ Fals	$125
1803	**Il-Kulug (fl.404h)**, Æ Fals	$150
1804	**Irtash (c.404-406h)**, Æ Fals	$150
1805	**Ilyas Hajjaj (fl.405h)**, Æ Fals	$150
1806	**Bars Oga (fl.406h)**, Æ Fals	$250
1807	**Bektuzun (fl.415h)**, Æ Fals	$250
1808	**Chaghri Subashi Uka (fl.417-426h)**, Æ Fals	$150
1809	**Anonymous**, BI Dirham	$100
1810	- Æ Fals	$50

GREAT SELJUQ

1811

| 1811 | **Tughril Beg (429-455h)**, AV Dinar (common mint: Nishapur) | $300 |

VF

1812	- AR Dirham	$1000
1813	**Chaghri Beg Da'ud (431-452h)**, AR Dirham	$250

1814

1815

1814	**Ibrahim b. Inanj Yabghu (c.434-441h)**, AV Dinar	$1200
1815	- AR Dirham	$600

1816

1816	**Bayghu (fl.434-448h)**, AV Dinar	$400

1817

1818

1817	**Alp Arslan, as governor at Herat (c.450-455h)**, AV Dinar	$300
1818	- **as sultan (455-465h)**, AV Dinar	$300
1819	**Takash Beg (c.454-477h)**, AV Dinar	$300
1820	**Arslan Shah, in Fars (c.458-461h)**, AV Dinar	*Extremely rare*

1821

1821	- **in Marw (c.464-467h)**, AV Dinar	$300
1822	**Malikshah (465-485h)**, AV Dinar, fine gold	$300

1823

		VF
1823	- AV Dinar, pale gold	$250
1824	- AV fractional Dinar	$750
1825	- AR Dirham	$300
1826	- Æ Fals	$125
1827	**Toghanshah (c.465-475h),** AV Dinar	$300
1828	**Mahmud I (485-487h),** AV Dinar	$750

1829

1829	**Arslan Arghu (486-490h),** AV Dinar	$400

1830

1830	**Barkiyaruq (486-498h),** AV Dinar	$300
1831	**Tutush b. Alp Arslan (fl.487-488h),** AV Dinar	$1500
1832	**Sanjar, as viceroy under Barkiyaruq (490-492h),** AV Dinar	$400

1833

1833	**Muhammad I (492-511h),** AV Dinar	$300
1834	**Sanjar, as viceroy under Muhammad I (492-511h),** AV Dinar	$300

1835

VF

| 1835 | **Sanjar (511-552h)**, AV Dinar | $300 |
| 1836 | **Mahmud b. Muhammad (549-557h)**, AR Dinar | *Extremely rare* |

SELJUQ OF HAMADAN

1837

| 1837 | **Shams al-Ma'ali Chaghri Takin (fl.467-484h)**, AV Dinar | $300 |
| 1838 | **Sayf al-dawla Inanj Beg (fl.486-491h)**, AV Dinar | $500 |

SELJUQ OF WESTERN IRAN

1839

1839	**Mahmud II (511-525h)**, AV Dinar	$400
1840	**Da'ud (525-526h)**, AV Dinar	*Extremely rare*
1841	**Tughril II (526-529h)**, AV Dinar	$500
1842	**Mas'ud (529-547h)**, AV Dinar	$500
1843	**Malikshah III (547-548h)**, AV Dinar	*Extremely rare*
1844	**Muhammad II (548-555h)**, AV Dinar	$500
1845	**Sulayman Shah, as viceroy (c.525-556h)**, AV Dinar	$500
1846	**Arslan (556-571h)**, AV Dinar	$300

SELJUQ OF KIRMAN

1847

1847	**Qara Arslan (440-465h),** AV Dinar	$400
1848	- AV ¼-Dinar	$500

1849

1849	- AR Dirham	$600
1850	**Sultanshah (467-477h),** AV Dinar	$750

1851

1851	**Turanshah I (477-490h),** AV Dinar	$500
1852	**Arslanshah I (495-537h),** AV Dinar, base gold	$300

AMIRS OF NISHAPUR

1853	**Ay-Aba (556-567h),** AV Dinar	$500
1854	**Toghanshah (567-581h),** AV Dinar	$500

ILDEGIZID

1855	**Shams al-din Ildegiz (531-571h),** BI Dirham	$75
1856	- Æ Fals	$60

	1857	VF
1857	**Pahlawan Muhammad (571-582h)**, Æ Fals	$60
1858	**Qizil Arslan 'Uthman (582-587h)**, Æ Fals	$150
1859	**Abu Bakr b. Muhammad (587-607h)**, Æ Fals	$60
1860	**Uzbek b. Muhammad (607-622h)**, Æ Fals	$80

ILDEGIZID VASSALS

1861	**Badkin b. Muhammad (c.600h)**, Æ Fals	$80

SULAMID

1862	**Muzaffar b. Muhammad (c.530-555h)**, Æ Fals	$100
1863	**Bikbars b. Muzaffar (566-585h)**, Æ Fals	$100
1864	**'Abd al-Malik b. Bikbars (585-600h)**, Æ Fals	$150

KHAQANID

1865	**Salar b. Yazid (441-455h)**, BI Dirham	$200
1866	**Fariburz I b. Salar (c.455-489h)**, BI Dirham	$125
1867	**Minuchihr III b. Afridun (c.514-555h)**, BI Dirham	$100
1868	**Akhsatan I b. Minuchihr (c.555-593h)**, Æ Dirham	$100
1869	**Shahanshah b. Minuchihr (c.575-600h)**, Æ Dirham	$200

1870   1871

1870	**Fariburz II b. Afridun (c.583-600h)**, Æ Fals	$125
1871	**Gershasp b. Farrukhzad (c.600-630h)**, Æ Fals	$75
1872	**Fariburz III b. Gershasp (c.622-641h)**, Æ Fals	$100
1873	**Akhsatan III b. Fariburz III (c.653-665h)**, Æ Fals	$250

PISHKINID

		VF
1874	**Pishkin II (c.591-601h),** Æ Dirham	$100
1875	**Mahmud b. Pishkin (c.608-623h),** Æ Dirham	$75

BATINID (Assassins of Alamut)

1876

1876	**Muhammad I (532-557h),** AV fractional Dinar	$2500
1877	*temp.* **al-Hasan II (557-561h),** AV fractional Dinar	$4000
1878	**'Ala al-din Muhammad III (618-653h),** AV Dinar	$4000

1879   1881

1879	- AV fractional Dinar	$2000
1880	- AR Dirham	*Extremely rare*
1881	- AR fractional Dirham	$1200

ATABEGS OF FARS

| 1882 | **Saljuqshah (c.517-524h),** AV Dinar | $500 |

1883

| 1883 | **Mankubars (c.524-533h),** AV Dinar | $500 |
| 1884 | **Boz-Aba (c.533-543h),** AV Dinar | $500 |

SALGHURID

1885

		VF
1885	**Sunqur (543-556h)**, AV Dinar	$400
1886	**Zangi (556-570h)**, AV Dinar	$300
1887	**Takla (570-590h)**, AV Dinar	$400
1888	**Tughril b. Sunqur (c.570-599h)**, AV Dinar	$1000
1889	**Abu Bakr (628-658h)**, AR Dirham	$800
1890	- Pb Fals	$1000

1891

1891	**Abish bint Sa'd (663-684h)**, AV Dinar	$400
1892	- AR Dirham	$150
1893	- AR Dirham, with Chinese character Bao	$1500
1894	- Æ Fals	$125
1895	- Æ Fals, with Chinese character Bao	$750

KHWARIZMSHAHS

1896	**Atsiz (521-551h)**, AV Dinar	$500
1897	**Il-Arslan (551-567h)**, AV Dinar	$400
1898	**Takash (567-596h)**, AV Dinar	$300

1899

1899	**'Ala al-din Muhammad (596-617h)**, AV Dinar	$250
1900	- AV Dinar, base gold, small flan	$80

1901

VF

1901   - AR Dirham $75

1902

1902   - Æ Dirham $50
1903   - Æ Fals $40

1904

1904   - Æ Jital $25
1905   **Jalal al-din Mangubarni (617-628h),** AV Dinar   *Extremely rare*
1906   - AR double Dirham $600
1907   - AR Dirham $300
1908   - BI Dirham, broad flan $400
1909   - Æ Fals $150
1910   - Æ Jital $50

AMIR OF BALKH

1911   **Abu'l-Mujahid Muhammad (fl.617-618h),** Æ Dirham $80

AMIRS OF WAKHSH

1912   **'Imad al-din Abu Bakr (c.597-609h),** AV Dinar $500
1913   **'Arabshah b. Abu Bakr (c.609-618h),** AV Dinar $750

1914

VF

1914   **Abu'l-'Abbas Muhammad b. Ahmad (fl.618h)**, AV Dinar $250

GHORID

1915   **Ghiyath al-din Muhammad b. Sam (558-599h)**, AV Dinar   *Extremely rare*

1916   - Æ Jital $50

1917   1918

1917   **Mu'izz al-din Muhammad b. Sam (567-602h)**, AV Dinar $400

1918   - AV Stater $200

1919

1919   - AR Dirham $75

1920   - Æ Jital $25

1921

1921   **Ghiyath al-din Mahmud (602-609h)**, AV Dinar $400

1922   - Æ Jital $50

1923

		VF
1923	**Taj al-din Yildiz (602-612h),** AV Dinar, fine gold	$500
1924	- AV Dinar, base gold	$250
1925	- AR Dirham	$80

1926

1926	- Æ Jital	$30

GHORID OF BAMIYAN

1927

1927	**Fakhr al-din Mas'ud (540-558h),** AR Dinar	$200
1928	**Shams al-din Muhammad (558-588h),** AV Dinar	$750
1929	- AR Dirham	$80
1930	**Baha' al-din Sam (588-602h),** AV Dinar	$500
1931	- AR Dirham	$50
1932	- BI Jital	$50

1933

1933	**Jalal al-din 'Ali (602-611h),** AV Dinar	$500
1934	- BI Dirham	$125
1935	- Æ Jital	$50

QARLUGHID

		1936	VF
1936	**al-Hasan Qarlugh (621-647h)**, AR Tanka		$150
1937	- Æ Jital		$25
1938	**Nasir al-din Muhammad (647-658h)**, AR Dirham		*Extremely rare*[4]

1939

1939	- Æ Jital	$25

IRAN, AFGHANISTAN, & CENTRAL ASIA
AFTER THE MONGOL INVASION

The lands conquered by the Mongols were soon divided between three dynasties, each founded by descendants of Chingiz (Genghis) Khan: the Chaghatayids in Central Asia, the Golden Horde in Khwarizm and southern Russia, and the Ilkhanids in Iran. The Chagatayids ruled until the rise of Timur in the late 8th century AH, and the Golden Horde until the early 10th century when their already much-reduced empire was conquered by the Giray Khans of the Crimea. Finally, the Ilkhanid empire lasted until the mid 8th century, after which Iran was once more divided into various smaller states. This was only temporary, however, because Timur conquered most of Iran by the end of the 8th century. The Timurid empire briefly spanned all of Iran and Central Asia, but their control began to weaken in the mid 9th century, and the Qara Qoyunlu and Aq Qoyunlu were able to take power in western Iran while a smaller Timurid kingdom remained in the east. In the early 10th century the Safavids conquered the Aq Qoyunlu kingdom and would go on to unite Iran once more.

Album, S., *Sylloge of Islamic Coins in the Ashmolean, Volume 9: Iran after the Mongol Invasion*, Oxford, 2001

GREAT MONGOL

1940

		VF
1940	**Chingiz Khan (603-624h),** AV Dinar	$5000

1941

1941	- AR Dirham	$1000
1942	- BI Dirham, broad flan	$1500
1943	*temp.* **Chingiz Khan,** AV Dinar	$1000
1944	- AR Dirham	$500
1945	- Æ Dirham	$200

1946

1946	- Æ Jital	$100

1947   **VF**

1947   *temp.* **Ögedei (624-639h)**, AV Dinar $5000

1948

| 1948 | - AR Dirham | $500 |
| 1949 | **Mas'ud al-Khwarizmi (fl.638-667h)**, Æ Fals | $150 |

1950

1950	*temp.* **Töregene (639-644h)**, AR Dirham, archer type	$2500
1951	- AR ½-Dirham, archer type	$800
1952	*temp.* **Güyük (644-647h)**, AR Dirham	$1000
1953	- AR ½-Dirham	$600
1954	**Möngke (649-658h)**, AV Dinar	$1500

1955

1955	- AR Dirham	$300
1956	- AR ½-Dirham	*Extremely rare*[1]
1957	- Æ Dirham	$250
1958	- Æ Fals	$400
1959	- Æ Jital	$150
1960	*temp.* **Arigh Buqa (658-662h)**, AR Dirham	$1000
1961	**Anonymous,** AR Dirham	$80

---

[1]   Stephen Album Rare Coins, Auction 18, 16-18 January 2014, lot 547

		VF
1962	- AR ½-Dirham	*Extremely rare*
1963	- Æ Dirham	$250
1964	- Æ Jital	$125

MALIK OF KURZUWAN

1965

1965	**Anonymous,** Æ Jital	$75

CHAGHATAYID

1966	*temp.* **Chaghatay (624-639h),** AV Dinar	$7500
1967	- AR Dirham	$800
1968	*temp.* **Qara Hulagu (639-645h),** AR Dirham	$500
1969	*temp.* **Yesu Möngke (645-650h),** AR Dirham	$500
1970	*temp.* **Orqina Khatun (650-659h),** AR Dirham	$300

1971

1971	*temp.* **Alughu (659-664h),** AR Dirham	$300
1972	*temp.* **Baraq (664-670h),** AR Dirham	$600
1973	**Anonymous,** AR Dirham, undated	$200

1974   1976

1974	*temp.* **Tuqa Timur (c.670-690h),** AR Dirham	$150
1975	*temp.* **Duwa Khan (c.690-706h),** AR Dirham	$250
1976	**Qutlugh Khwaja (fl.697-698h),** Æ Jital	$40
1977	*temp.* **Isan Buqa (708-718h),** AR Dirham	$250
1978	**Kibak Khan (718-726h),** AR Dinar	$250

1979

		VF
1979	- AR 1/6-Dinar	$75
1980	*temp*. **Ilchigiday (726-727h)**, AR Dinar	$300
1981	- AR 1/6-Dinar	$125
1982	**Tarmashirin (726-734h)**, AR Dinar, in his name	$300
1983	- AR Dinar, anonymous	$200
1984	- AR 1/6-Dinar	$150
1985	**Sanjar (731-734h)**, AR Dinar	$300
1986	**Changshi (734-737h)**, AR 1/6-Dinar	$125

1987

1987	**Yesun Timur (737-741h)**, AR Dinar	$125
1988	- AR 1/6-Dinar	$150
1989	**Muhammad (741-742h)**, AR Dinar	$500
1990	**Khalil (742-744h)**, AR Dinar	$250

1991

1991	**Qazan Timur (744-747h)**, AR Dinar	$250
1992	**Dashmand Shah (747-749h)**, AR Dinar	$250
1993	**Buyan Quli Khan (749-760h)**, AR Dinar	$150
1994	- AR 12-Dirhams	$275

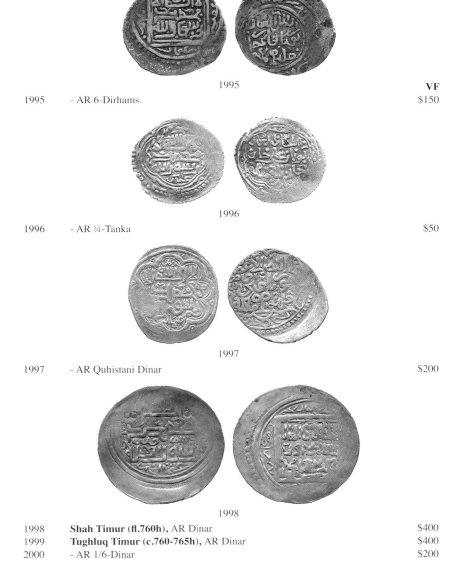

		1995	**VF**
1995	- AR 6-Dirhams		$150

1996

| 1996 | - AR ¼-Tanka | $50 |

1997

| 1997 | - AR Quhistani Dinar | $200 |

1998

1998	**Shah Timur (fl.760h),** AR Dinar	$400
1999	**Tughluq Timur (c.760-765h),** AR Dinar	$400
2000	- AR 1/6-Dinar	$200

2001

		VF
2001	**Qabul Khan (fl.767-769h),** AR 1/6-Dinar	$150
2002	**Suyurghatmish (771-790h),** AR 1/6-Dinar	$300
2003	**Anonymous,** Æ Fals	$100

SHAHS OF BADAKHSHAN

2004

2004	**Dawlatshah (fl.690-693h),** AR Dirham	$200
2005	- AR ½-Dirham	$250
2006	**Arghunshah (fl.706-711h),** AR Dirham	$300
2007	**Sultan Bakht (fl.711-715h),** AR Dirham	$250
2008	**'Alishah II (fl.717-718h),** AR Dirham	$150
2009	**Shah Baha' al-din (fl.745-761h),** AR Dinar Kebeki	$400
2010	**Bahramshah (fl.769-776h),** AR 1/6-Dinar	$100

GOLDEN HORDE

2011	**Anonymous,** AR Dinar, citing the caliph al-Nasir	$500

2012

2012	- AR Dirham, citing Möngke	$150
2013	- AR Dirham, citing Arigh Buqa	$500
2014	- AR Dirham	$100
2015	- AR ½-Dirham	$150
2016	- AR 1/5-Dirham	$100
2017	- Æ Pul, citing Möngke	$200
2018	**Nusrat al-din Berke (655-665h),** AR Yarmaq	$1500
2019	- Æ Fals	$200
2020	**Mangu Timur (665-679h),** AR Dirham	$200

2021

		VF
2021	**Toda Mangu (679-686h),** AR Dirham, in his name	$150
2022	- AR Dirham, anonymous	$150

2023

2023	**Töle Buqa (686-689h),** AR Dirham, in his name	$150
2024	- AR Dirham, anonymous	$125

2025

2025	**Toqtu (689-712h),** AR Dirham	$100
2026	- Æ Pul	$100

2027

2027	**Muhammad Uzbek (712-742h),** AR Dirham	$60
2028	- Æ Pul	$75

2029

2029	**Jani Beg (742-758h),** AR Dinar	$150
2030	- AR ¼-Tanka	$100

		2031	**VF**
2031	- AR Dirham		$50
2032	- Æ Pul		$100

2033   **2034**

2033	**Birdi Beg (758-761h),** AR Dirham	$75
2034	**Qulna Khan (760-761h),** AR Dirham	$125

2035   **2036**

2035	**Nawruz Beg (760-761h),** AR Dirham	$100
2036	**Khizr Khan (760-762h),** AR Dirham	$75
2037	**Timur Khwaja Khan (762h),** AR Dirham	$200

2038

2038	**Kildi Beg (762-763h),** AR Dirham	$125
2039	- Æ Pul	$100

2040

2040	**Murid Khan (762-764h),** AR Dirham	$125
2041	**Khayr Pulad Khan (764h),** AR Dirham	$200

2042

VF
Extremely rare

2042   - Æ Pul

2043   2044

2043	**'Abd Allah Khan (762-771h)**, AR Dirham	$75
2044	**'Aziz Shaykh (766-768h)**, AR Dirham	$150
2045	**Urus Khan (fl.770-779h)**, AR Dirham	$250

2046   2048

2046	**Muhammad Bulaq Khan (771-782h)**, AR Dirham	$75
2047	**Tulun Beg (773h)**, Æ Pul	$150
2048	**Toqtamish (778-797h)**, AR Dirham	$50
2049	- Æ Pul	$125
2050	**Tulak (fl.782h)**, AR Dirham	$200

2051

2051	**Beg Pulad Khan (792-794h)**, AR Dirham	$250
2052	**Tashtimur (fl.796-799h)**, AR Dirham	$250
2053	**Timur Qutlugh (797-803h)**, AR Dirham	$150
2054	**Shadi Beg (803-810h)**, AR Tanka	$250

2055

2055	- AR Dirham	$125
2056	**Pulad Khan (810-813h)**, AR Dirham	$100
2057	**Timur Khan (813-814h)**, AR Dirham	$250
2058	**Ulugh Muhammad (821-828h)**, AR Dirham	$100
2059	**Beg Sufi (fl.822-824h)**, AR Dirham	$250

		VF
2060	**Dawlat Birdi Khan (827-840h),** AR Dirham	$125
2061	**Mustafa Khan (fl.847h),** AR Dirham	$250
2062	**Anonymous,** Æ Pul	$25

KHANATE OF SAQCHI

2063	**Noghay (d. 699h),** AR Dirham	$500

ILKHANID

Diler, O., *Ilkhans: Coinage of the Persian Mongols,* Istanbul, 2006

2064	**Hulagu (654-663h),** AV Dinar, citing Möngke as overlord	$2500

2065

2065	- AR Dirham, citing Möngke as overlord	$300

2066

2066	- AR Dirham	$80
2067	- Æ Fals	$75

2068

2068	**Abaqa (663-680h),** AV Dinar	$600

2069

		VF
2069	- AV Dinar, citing Möngke as overlord	$2500
2070	- AR Dirham	$125
2071	- AR Dirham, lion on obverse	$300
2072	- Æ Fals	$50
2073	- Æ Jital	$250

2074

2074	**Anonymous,** AR Dirham	$75

2075

2075	**Ahmad Tekudar (681-683h),** AR Dirham	$150
2076	- Æ Fals	$100
2077	**Arghun (683-690h),** AV Dinar	$500
2078	- AV Dinar, hawk on reverse	$2500

2079   2080

2079	- AR Dirham, standard type	$60
2080	- AR Dirham, hawk on reverse	$100
2081	- AR Dirham, lion on obverse	$250

2082

		VF
2082	- AR Dirham, local types	$80
2083	- AR ½-Dirham	$125
2084	- AR ¼-Dirham	$100
2085	- Æ Fals	$50

2086

2086	**Gaykhatu (690-694h),** AV Dinar	$400

2087

2087	- AR Dirham	$60
2088	- AR Dirham, lion on reverse	$200
2089	- Æ Fals	$100
2090	**Baydu (694h),** AV Dinar	$500

2091

2091	- AR Dirham	$100
2092	- Æ Fals	$150
2093	**Ghazan Mahmud (694-703h),** AV Dinar, pre-reform	$500
2094	- AR Dirham, pre-reform	$80
2095	- AV Dinar, post-reform	$400

2096

		VF
2096	- AV Dinar, post-reform, with additional marginal legends on both sides	$3000

2097

| 2097 | - AR Dinar, post-reform | $1000 |

2098

| 2098 | - AR 2-Dirhams, post-reform | $60 |

2099

2099	- AR Dirham, post-reform	$40
2100	- AR ½-Dirham, post-reform	$150
2101	- AR Dirham, local types	$100
2102	- Æ Fals	$50
2103	- Æ 'Adliya	$300
2104	**Uljaytu (703-716h),** AV Dinar, type A	$800
2105	- AR 6-Dirhams, type A	$1500

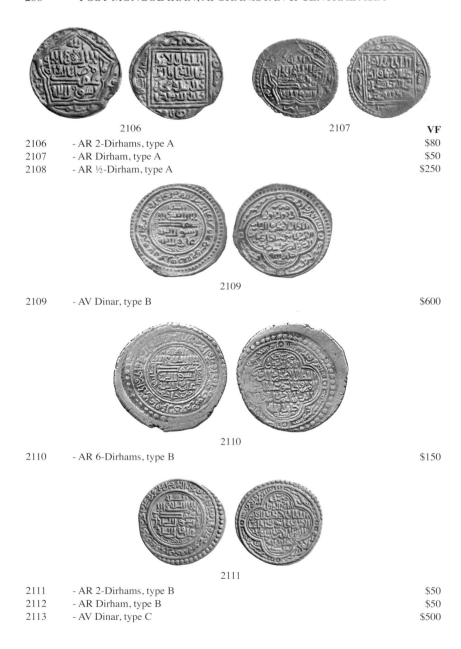

		2106	**2107**	**VF**
2106	- AR 2-Dirhams, type A			$80
2107	- AR Dirham, type A			$50
2108	- AR ½-Dirham, type A			$250

2109

2109	- AV Dinar, type B	$600

2110

2110	- AR 6-Dirhams, type B	$150

2111

2111	- AR 2-Dirhams, type B	$50
2112	- AR Dirham, type B	$50
2113	- AV Dinar, type C	$500

2114

2114   - AR 6-Dirhams, type C $125

2115

2115   - AR 6-Dirhams, type C, with additional marginal legends on both sides $300

2116

2116	- AR 2-Dirhams, type C	$40
2117	- AR Dirham, type C	$40
2118	- AR ½-Dirham, type C	$125
2119	- Æ Fals	$30
2120	- Æ 'Adliya	$100
2121	**Abu Sa'id (716-736h),** AV Dinar, type A	$750
2122	- AR 2-Dirhams, type A	$100
2123	- AR Dirham, type A	$50
2124	- AV Dinar, type B	$500
2125	- AR 6-Dirhams, type B	$150

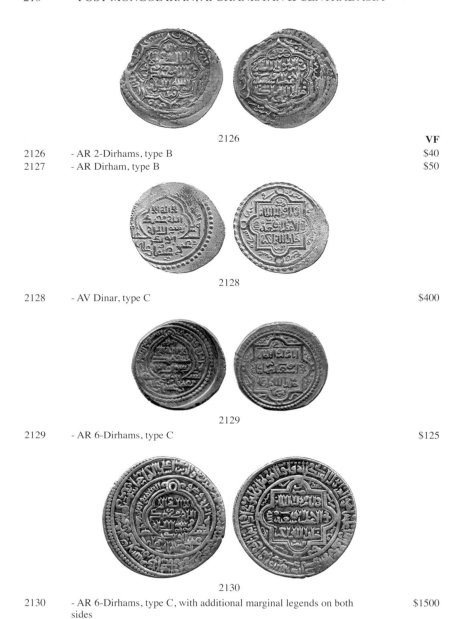

2126   **VF**

2126   - AR 2-Dirhams, type B $40
2127   - AR Dirham, type B $50

2128

2128   - AV Dinar, type C $400

2129

2129   - AR 6-Dirhams, type C $125

2130

2130   - AR 6-Dirhams, type C, with additional marginal legends on both $1500
         sides

2131

2132

2131	- AR 2-Dirhams, type C	$30
2132	- AR Dirham, type C	$40

2133

2133	- AV Dinar, type D	$400
2134	- AR 6-Dirhams, type D	$125

2135

2138

2135	- AR 2-Dirhams, type D	$30
2136	- AR Dirham, type D	$30
2137	- AV Dinar, type E	$5000
2138	- AR 2-Dirhams, type E	$250

2139

2139	- AV Dinar, type F	$400

2140

2140   - AR 6-Dirhams, type F $150

2141   2143

2141	- AR 2-Dirhams, type F	$25
2142	- AR Dirham, type F	$30
2143	- AV Dinar, type G	$400
2144	- AR 6-Dirhams, type G	$125

2145   2148

2145	- AR 2-Dirhams, type G	$25
2146	- AR Dirham, type G	$30
2147	- AV Dinar, type H	$500
2148	- AR 6-Dirhams, type H	$125

2149

2149	- AR 2-Dirhams, type H	$25
2150	- AR Dirham, type H	$30
2151	- Æ Fals	$80

2152

2153

VF

| 2152 | **Arpa Khan (736h),** AV Dinar | $8000 |
| 2153 | - AR 2-Dirhams | $500 |

2154

2155

2154	**Musa Khan (736-737h),** AV Dinar	$10,000
2155	- AR 2-Dirhams	$500
2156	- Æ Fals	$600
2157	**Muhammad (736-738h),** AV Dinar	$2500
2158	- AV ½-Mithqal	$1200

2159

2160

| 2159 | - AR 6-Dirhams | $80 |
| 2160 | - AR 4-Dirhams | $125 |

2161

2161	- AR 2-Dirhams	$30
2162	- AR Dirham	$50
2163	- Æ Fals	$50
2164	**Taghay Timur (737-754h),** AV Dinar	$750

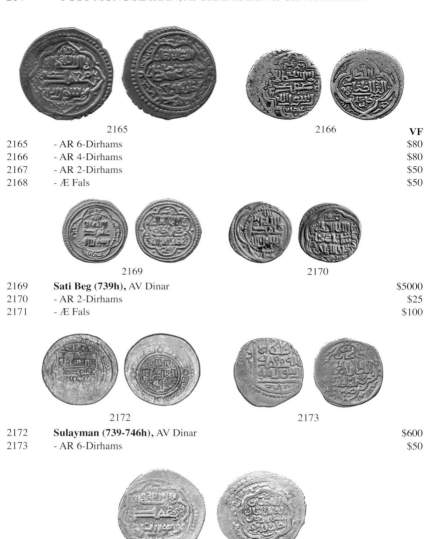

		2165		2166	**VF**
2165	- AR 6-Dirhams				$80
2166	- AR 4-Dirhams				$80
2167	- AR 2-Dirhams				$50
2168	- Æ Fals				$50

		2169		2170	
2169	**Sati Beg (739h),** AV Dinar				$5000
2170	- AR 2-Dirhams				$25
2171	- Æ Fals				$100

		2172		2173	
2172	**Sulayman (739-746h),** AV Dinar				$600
2173	- AR 6-Dirhams				$50

2174

2174	- AR 4-Dirhams	$125

2175

		VF
2175	- AR 2-Dirhams	$15
2176	- AR Dirham	$75
2177	- Æ Fals	$50
2178	**Jahan Timur (740-741h)**, AV Dinar	*Extremely rare*[2]
2179	- AR 2-Dirhams	$100
2180	**Anushiravan (745-757h)**, AV Dinar	$1500
2181	- AR 6-Dirhams	$100
2182	- AR 4-Dirhams	*Extremely rare*

2183

2183	- AR 2-Dirhams	$40
2184	- Æ Fals	$100
2185	**Ghazan II (757-758h)**, AR 6-Dirhams	$150
2186	- AR 2-Dirhams	$75

QUTLUGHKHANID

2187

2187	**Qutlugh Turkan (655-681h)**, AV Dinar	$800
2188	**Suyurghatmish (681-693h)**, AV Dinar	$1200
2189	- AR Dirham	$250
2190	**Padishah Khatun (693-694h)**, AV Dinar	$1500
2191	- AR Dirham	$300

---

[2] Morton & Eden Auction 54, 23 April 2012, lot 153

	2192	2193	VF
2192	**Shah Jahan, 1ˢᵗ reign (694h)**, AV Dinar		$1500
2193	- AR Dirham		$300

2194

2194	**Shah Sultan (694-702h)**, AR Dirham	$150

ATABEGS OF YAZD

2195	**Yusufshah (684-696h)**, AV Dinar	$1500
2196	- AR Dirham	$150

ATABEGS OF SHABANKARA

2197	**Isma'il b. Muhammad (c.680h)**, AV Dinar	$1500

QALHATI AMIRS OF HORMUZ

2198	**Nusrat Shah (c.677-689h)**, AV Dinar	*Extremely rare*
2199	*temp.* **Turanshah II (c.840-860h)**, AV fractional Dinar	$250
2200	*temp.* **Mas'ud (860-871h)**, AV fractional Dinar	$500
2201	**Sayf al-din (913-919h)**, AR Dirham	$250
2202	**Turanshah III (919-928h)**, AV Dinar	$300
2203	- AR Dirham	$150
2204	**Muhammad (928-941h)**, AV Dinar, countermarked type	$500
2205	**Turanshah IV (948-971h)**, AV Dinar	$300
2206	- AR Dirham	$150

CHUPANID

2207	**Malik Ashraf (c.745-758h)**, AR Dinar	*Extremely rare*[3]

³   Stephen Album Rare Coins, Auction 10, 22-23 April 2011, lot 949

INJUYID

2208

		VF
2208	**Abu Ishaq (743-757h),** AV Dinar	$2500
2209	- AR Dinar	$50

HAZARASPID

2210

2210	*temp.* **Nur-Award (751-757h),** AR Dinar	$60

MUZAFFARID

2211	**Muhammad b. al-Muzaffar (736-759h),** AR Dinar	$50
2212	**Mahmud b. Muhammad (759-776h),** AR Dinar	$100

2213   2214

2213	**Shah Shuja' (759-786h),** AR 2-Dinars	$30
2214	- AR Dinar	$25
2215	- Æ Fals	$40
2216	**Zayn al-'Abidin (786-789, 790-793h),** AR 2-Dinars	$40

2217

2217	**Shah Mansur (790-795h),** AR 2-Dinars	$30

JALAYRID

2219   **VF**

2218	*temp.* **Shaykh Hasan (736-757h)**, AV Dinar	$2000
2219	- AR Dinar	$40
2220	- AR 1/3-Dinar	$50

2221   2222

2221	**Shaykh Uways I (757-776h)**, AV Dinar	$1500
2222	- AR 2-Dinars	$50

2223

2223	- AR Dinar	$25
2224	- AR Dinar, countermarked type	$30
2225	- Æ Fals	$40

2226   2228

2226	**Sultan Husayn I (776-784h)**, AV Dinar	$2000
2227	- AR 2-Dinars	$40
2228	- AR Dinar	$25
2229	- AR Dinar, countermarked type	$50

		2230		2232		VF

2230	**Sultan Ahmad, 1st reign (784-795h),** AV Dinar	$2000
2231	- AV fractional Dinar	$1500
2232	- AR 2-Dinars	$30
2233	- AR Dinar	$30

2234

2234	**Sultan Ahmad, 2nd reign (807-813h),** AR Tanka	$125
2235	- AR 1/3-Tanka	$75
2236	- AR 2-Dirhams	$30

SUTAYID

2237	*temp.* **Ibrahimshah (743-748h),** AR 2-Dirhams	$75

BUKHTI KURDS

2238	**'Abd Allah b. 'Abd Allah (c.820-830h),** AR Tanka	$150

2239

2239	**Badr al-din (c.870-880h),** AR Tanka	$150

SHARAF KHANS

2240

		VF
2240	**Sharaf b. Muhammad (c.815-820h),** AR Tanka	$300

2241

2241	**Shams al-din b. Diya' al-din (c.850h),** AR Tanka	$300
2242	**Ibrahim b. Muhammad (fl.865-871h),** AR Tanka	$400

HUSAYNID

2243	*temp.* **Sayyid Rida Kiya (798-829h),** AR Tanka	$125

AFRASIYABID

2244	**Anonymous,** AV Dinar, in the name of al-Mahdi Muhammad	*Extremely rare*
2245	- AR 6-Dirhams, in the name of al-Mahdi Muhammad	$125
2246	- AR 4-Dirhams, in the name of al-Mahdi Muhammad	$125

SARBADARID

2247	*temp.* **Shams al-din 'Ali (748-752h),** AR Dinar	$300

2248

2248	*temp.* **Hasan Damghani (759-763h),** AR 6-Dirhams	$60
2249	- AR 2-Dirhams	$40
2250	*temp.* **'Ali Mu'ayyad (763-786h),** AV Tanka	*Extremely rare*

2251

		VF
2251	- AV ½-Mithqal	$250
2252	- AR 6-Dirhams	$40
2253	- AR 4-Dirhams	$40
2254	- AR 2-Dirhams	$50
2255	- AR Dirham	$40
2256	- Æ Fals	$30

WALID

2257

2257	*temp.* **Amir Wali (757-788h),** AR 6-Dirhams	$30
2258	- AR 4-Dirhams	$25
2259	- AR 3-Dirhams	$40

TAGHAYTIMURID

2260	**Pir Muhammad b. Luqman (790-812h),** AR heavy Tanka	$250
2261	- AR light Tanka	$150
2262	- AR ½-Tanka	*Extremely rare*

KART

2263	**Mu'izz al-din Husayn (732-771h),** AR ½-Tanka	$250

2264

2264	- AR ¼-Tanka	$150
2265	*temp.* **Mu'izz al-din Husayn,** AR ½-Tanka	$300

	2266	**VF**
2266	- AR 12-Dirhams	$150

2267

2267	- AR 6-Dirhams	$150
2268	- AR 3-Dirhams	$200
2269	*temp*. **Pir 'Ali (771-784h)**, AV Mithqal	*Extremely rare*[4]
2270	- AR 12-Dirhams	$150

2271

2271	- AR Tanka	$125

MEHRABANID

2272

		VF
2272	**Nasir al-din Muhammad b. Abi'l-Fath (659-718h)**, AR Dinar	$150
2273	- Æ Fals (cast)	$150
2274	**al-Malik b. Nasr (c.670-680h)**, Æ Fals (cast)	$150
2275	**Nusrat al-din Muhammad (c.718-731h)**, AR Dinar	$250
2276	**Qutb al-din Muhammad I (731-747h)**, Æ Jital	$40
2277	**Yamin al-din Mahmud (751-753h)**, Æ Jital	$75

2278

2278	**'Izz al-din Karman (753-784h)**, AV Tanka	$750
2279	- AR Dinar	$250
2280	- Æ Jital	$25
2281	**Qutb al-din Muhammad II (784-788h)**, AV Tanka	$1000

2282

2282	**Qutb al-din Muhammad 'Ali (806-822h)**, AR Tanka	$200
2283	- Æ Fals	*Extremely rare*

SUFID

2284

2284	*temp.* **Husayn (762-774h)**, AV fractional Dinar	$300

VF

2285	- AR Dirham	$100
2286	- Æ Pul	$75
2287	*temp*. **Yusuf (774-781h),** AV fractional Dinar	$400
2288	- AR Dirham	$100
2289	- Æ Pul	$75

TIMURID

2290	**Timur (771-807h),** AV fractional Dinar	$800

2291

2291	- AR Dinar Kebeki	$200

2292

2292	- AR Tanka, pre-reform coinage	$150
2293	- AR 4-Dinars, pre-reform	$75
2294	- AR 2-Dinars, pre-reform	$60
2295	- AR 4-Dirhams, pre-reform	$60

2296   2298

2296	- AR Dirham, pre-reform	$40
2297	- AR Akçe, pre-reform	$60
2298	- AR Tanka, post-reform coinage	$100
2299	- AR ¼-Tanka, post-reform	$125

2300 2301

		VF
2300	- AR Tanka, countermarked type	$50
2301	- Æ Fals	$30
2302	**Khalil Sultan (807-811h)**, AR Tanka	$200
2303	- AR Tanka, countermarked type	$200
2304	- AR ¼-Tanka	$75
2305	**Pir Muhammad b. Jahangir (807-808h)**, AR Tanka	$150
2306	**Iskandar (812-817h)**, AR Tanka	$125
2307	- AR Tanka, countermarked type	$75
2308	**Pir Muhammad b. 'Umar Shaykh (807-812h)**, AR Tanka	$150
2309	**Rustam (c.812-817h)**, AR Tanka	$250

2310

2310	**Shahrukh (807-850h)**, AR Tanka	$25

2311 2312

2311	- AR Tanka, countermarked type	$25
2312	- AR ¼-Tanka	$50
2313	**Qaydu (808-811h)**, AR ¼-Tanka	$200

2314

2314	**Sultan Muhammad (850-855h)**, AR Tanka	$75
2315	- AR Tanka, countermarked type	$75

	2316	2317	**VF**

2316	**Abu Bakr (851h)**, AR Tanka	$200
2317	**'Ala al-dawla (851h)**, AR Tanka	$150
2318	- AR ¼-Tanka	$250

2319

| 2319 | **Abu'l-Qasim Babur (851-861h)**, AR Tanka | $40 |
| 2320 | - AR ¼-Tanka | $80 |

	2321	2323	

2321	**Ulugh Beg I (851-853h)**, AR Tanka	$125
2322	**'Abd al-Latif (853-854h)**, AR Tanka	$200
2323	**'Abd Allah (854-855h)**, AR Tanka	$80
2324	**Abu Sa'id (855-873h)**, AV ½-Mithqal	*Extremely rare*[5]

	2325	2328	

2325	- AR Tanka	$30
2326	- AR Tanka, countermarked type	$40
2327	- AR ¼-Tanka	$75
2328	**Sultan Ibrahim (861h)**, AR Tanka	$275

2329

2330

VF

2329	**Shah Mahmud (861-863h),** AR Tanka	$100
2330	- AR ¼-Tanka	*Extremely rare*

2331

2331	**Sultan Husayn, 1st reign (862-864h),** AR Tanka	$200
2332	**Sultan Husayn, 2nd reign (865-868h),** AR Tanka	$300
2333	**Yadigar Muhammad (873-875h),** AR Tanka, countermarked type	$125

2334

2335

2334	**Sultan Husayn, 3rd reign (873-911h),** AR Tanka	$25
2335	- AR Tanka, countermarked type	$25

2336

2336	- AR ½-Tanka	$75
2337	- AR ¼-Tanka	$100
2338	- AR 2-Miri	$100
2339	**Ulugh Beg Kabuli (873-907h),** AR Tanka, countermarked type	$150
2340	**Sultan Ahmad (873-899h),** AR Tanka	$100

2341

		VF
2341	- AR Tanka, countermarked type	$50

2342

2342	**Sultan Mahmud, 2ⁿᵈ reign (873-900h)**, AR Tanka	$125
2343	- AR Tanka, countermarked type	$100
2344	**Sultan Mas'ud, at Hisar (899-906h)**, AR Tanka, countermarked type	$125
2345	**Baysunghur (900-903h)**, AR Tanka, countermarked type	$60

2346

2346	**Sultan 'Ali (900-905h)**, AR Tanka, countermarked type	$75

2347

2347	**Muhammad b. Husayn, rebel (903-906h)**, AR Tanka	$60
2348	- AR Tanka, countermarked type	$50
2349	**Badi' al-Zaman, as rebel (c.905-908h)**, AR Tanka, countermarked type	$60
2350	**Faridun Husayn (911-912h)**, AR Tanka	$300

2351

		VF
2351	- AR Tanka, countermarked type	$150
2352	**Muhammad Muhsin Khan (911-912h)**, AR Tanka	$300

2353

| 2353 | **Badi' al-Zaman (911-914h)**, AR 3-Tankas, countermarked type | $125 |

SHIRVANSHAHS

2354	*temp.* **Kayka'us (745-774h)**, AR Dinar	$50
2355	*temp.* **Ibrahim I (784-821h)**, AR Tanka	$100
2356	*temp.* **Khalil Allah I (821-869h)**, AR Tanka	$40
2357	**Farrukhsiyar (869-906h)**, AR Tanka	$30
2358	**Ibrahim II (908-930h)**, AR Akçe	$30
2359	**Khalil Allah II (930-942h)**, AR Akçe	$25
2360	**Shahrukh (942-945h)**, AR Akçe	$75

QARA QOYUNLU

2361   2363

2361	**Qara Yusuf, 2ⁿᵈ reign (809-823h)**, AR Tanka	$150
2362	- AR 1/3-Tanka	$75
2363	- AR Akçe	$75

2364	2365	VF
2364	**Pir Budaq I (814-821h)**, AR ¼-Tanka	$50
2365	**Pir 'Umar, rebel (822-823h)**, AR Akçe, countermarked type	$50

2366

2366	**Iskandar (823-841h)**, AR Tanka	$50
2367	- AR Tanka, anonymous countermarked type	$100
2368	*temp.* **Aspan (837-844h)**, AR heavy Tanka	$400

2369		2370	
2369	- AR ¼-Tanka		$200
2370	**Jahanshah (841-872h)**, AR Tanka		$40

2371

2371	- AR Tanka, countermarked type	$50
2372	- AR ¼-Tanka	$50
2373	**Hasan 'Ali (872-873h)**, AR Tanka, countermarked type	$50

AQ QOYUNLU

2374	**'Uthman (780-839h)**, AR Akçe	$80
2375	**Hamza (839-848h)**, AR light Tanka	$50
2376	- AR Akçe	$200
2377	**Jahangir (848-857h)**, Æ Fals	$100

2378

		VF
2378	**Hasan (857-882h),** AV Ashrafi	$500
2379	- AR Tanka	$30

2380   2381

2380	- AR Tanka, countermarked type	$30
2381	- AR ¼-Tanka	$60
2382	**Khalil (882-883h),** AR Tanka	$200
2383	**Ya'qub (883-896h),** AV Ashrafi	$500

2384   2386

2384	- AR Tanka	$30
2385	- AR light Tanka	$25
2386	- AR Tanka, countermarked type	$25
2387	- AR ¼-Tanka	$25
2388	**Baysunghur (896-897h),** AV Ashrafi	$600

2389   2390

2389	- AR Tanka	$50
2390	- AR 2/5-Tanka	$40

2391

2391	- AR Tanka, countermarked type	$40

			VF
2392	**Rustam (897-902h),** AV Ashrafi		$500
2393	- AV Ashrafi, countermarked type		$600
2394	- AR Tanka		$30

2395

2395	- AR Tanka, countermarked type		$40
2396	- AR light Tanka		$30
2397	- AR 2/5-Tanka		$25

2398

2398	- AR 2/5-Tanka, countermarked type		$25
2399	**Ahmad (902-903h),** AR Tanka		$50
2400	**Muhammad (903-905h),** AR Tanka		$150

2401

2401	- AR 1/5-Tanka, countermarked type		$30
2402	**Alvand (903-910h),** AR Tanka		$50
2403	- AR 2/5-Tanka		$30
2404	**Qasim (903-908h),** AR Tanka		$100
2405	- AR 2/5-Tanka		$50
2406	**Murad (905-914h),** AR Tanka		$150
2407	- AR light Tanka		$40
2408	**Anonymous,** AR Tanka, countermarked type		$40
2409	- AR 2/5-Tanka, countermarked type		$30
2410	- Æ Fals		$60

MUSHA'SHA'

2411	**Fallah b. al-Muhsin (fl.905-906h),** AR ½-Tanka		$150

AMIR OF QUNDUZ

2412

		VF
2412	***temp.* Amir Khusraw (902-910h),** Æ 2-Dinars	$50
2413	- Æ Dinar, countermarked type	$50

INDIA

Although parts of Sind and the Punjab were under Muslim rule during the 3rd-5th centuries AH, the story of Muslim rule in India really begins with the Ghorid invasion of 587-588h and their capture of Dehli in 588h. After the death of the Ghorid ruler Mu'izz al-din Muhammad in 602h, the Ghorid lands in India soon became independent from the rest of the Ghorid kingdom, and the Dehli sultanate was born. Bengal was initially ruled by governors on behalf of the Dehli sultans, but the influence of Dehli was gradually weakened and eventually Bengal also became an independent sultanate. In the mid-8th century AH the focus of the Dehli sultans on military campaigns in the north enabled local rulers in the south to found first the Sultanate of Madura and then the Bahmanid sultanate. The Dehli sultanate was further weakened by Timur's invasion of India in 801h; this led to the foundation of the other four main sultanates of Jaunpur, Gujarat, Malwa, and Kashmir. The Indian sultanates were gradually subsumed into the nascent Mughal empire in the 10th century AH.

Goron, S., & Goenka, J.P., *The Coins of the Indian Sultanates*, New Delhi, 2001

HABBARID OF SIND

		VF
2414	**Da'ud,** AR Damma	$25
2415	**'Abd al-Rahman,** AR Damma	$15
2416	**'Abd Allah,** AR Damma	$10
2417	**'Ali,** AR Damma	$10
2418	**'Umar,** AR Damma	$10
2419	**Khatam,** AR Damma	$25
2420	**Yahya,** AR Damma	$40
2421	**'Isa,** AR Damma	$40
2422	**Muhammad,** AR Damma	$10
2423	**Ahmad,** AR Damma	$10
2424	**Ya'qub Beg,** AR Damma	$10

AMIRS OF MULTAN

2425	**Munabbih,** AR Damma	$40
2426	**Asad (fl.305h),** AR Damma	$40
2427	**Muhammad,** AR Damma	$25
2428	**Shibl,** AR Damma	$10

SULTANS OF SIND

2429	**Nasir al-din Qubacha (603-626h),** BI Jital	$20

SULTANS OF DEHLI

2430

<table>
<tr><td></td><td></td><td>VF</td></tr>
<tr><td>2430</td><td>Shams al-din Iltutmish (607-633h), AR Tanka</td><td>$200</td></tr>
<tr><td>2431</td><td>- BI Jital</td><td>$10</td></tr>
<tr><td>2432</td><td>- Æ 'Adli</td><td>$15</td></tr>
</table>

2433

<table>
<tr><td>2433</td><td>Rukn al-din Firuz (633-634h), AR Tanka</td><td>$250</td></tr>
<tr><td>2434</td><td>- BI Jital</td><td>$25</td></tr>
</table>

2435

<table>
<tr><td>2435</td><td>Jalalat al-din Radiyya (634-637h), AR Tanka</td><td>$400</td></tr>
<tr><td>2436</td><td>- BI Jital</td><td>$40</td></tr>
<tr><td>2437</td><td>Mu'izz al-din Bahram (637-639h), AV Tanka</td><td>Extremely rare[1]</td></tr>
</table>

---

[1]   Baldwin's Auction 53, 25 September 2007, lot 1561

2438

2438	- AR Tanka	$250
2439	- BI Jital	$25
2440	**'Ala al-din Mas'ud (639-644h)**, AV Tanka	*Extremely rare*

2441

2441	- AR Tanka	$75
2442	- BI Jital	$15

2443

2443	**Nasir al-din Mahmud (644-664h)**, AV Tanka	$800
2444	- AR Tanka	$60
2445	- BI Jital	$15
2446	- Æ 'Adli	$15

2447

2447	**Ghiyath al-din Balban (664-686h)**, AV Tanka	$600

2448

		VF
2448	- AR Tanka	$60
2449	- BI Dugani	$15
2450	- BI Jital	$30
2451	- Æ Paika	$15
2452	- Æ 'Adli	$25
2453	**Mu'izz al-din Kaiqubad (686-689h),** AV Tanka	$600

2454

2454	- AR Tanka	$75
2455	- BI 3-Gani	$15
2456	- Æ Paika	$15
2457	- Æ 'Adli	$25
2458	**Shams al-din Kayumarth (689h),** AR Tanka	$1500
2459	- Æ Paika	$75

2460

2460	**Jalal al-din Firuz (689-695h),** AV Tanka	$800
2461	- AR Tanka	$50
2462	- BI Jital	$15
2463	- Æ Paika	$15
2464	- Æ 'Adli	$25
2465	**Rukn al-din Ibrahim (695h),** AV Tanka	*Extremely rare*[2]

---

[2]   Heritage ANA Auction, Chicago, 8 August 2014, lot 23321

2466

		VF
2466	- AR Tanka	$1500
2467	- BI Jital	$40
2468	- Æ Paika	$40
2469	- Æ 'Adli	$50

2470

2470	**'Ala al-din Muhammad (695-715h),** AV Tanka	$600

2471

2471	- AR Tanka	$40
2472	- BI 6-Gani	$15
2473	- BI 2-Gani	$15
2474	- Æ Paika	$15
2475	- Æ 'Adli	$25
2476	**Shihab al-din 'Umar (715-716h),** AR Tanka	$1500
2477	- BI 6-Gani	$50
2478	**Qutb al-din Mubarak (716-720h),** AV Tanka	$1000

2479

2479   - AV square Tanka $2000

2480

2480   - AR Tanka $125

2481   2483

2481	- AR square Tanka	$250
2482	- BI 12-Gani	$30
2483	- BI 8-Gani	$25
2484	- BI 6-Gani	$15
2485	- BI 4-Gani	$15
2486	- Æ Paika	$30
2487	- Æ 'Adli	$30

2488

2488   **Nasir al-din Khusru (720h),** AV Tanka $3000
2489   - AR Tanka $1500

2490   **VF**

2490	- BI 12-Gani	$50
2491	- BI 6-Gani	$40
2492	- BI 2-Gani	$30
2493	- Æ Paika	$30

2494

| 2494 | **Ghiyath al-din Tughluq (720-725h),** AV Tanka | $800 |

2495

| 2495 | - AR Tanka | $75 |

2496   2497

2496	- BI 6-Gani	$25
2497	- BI 4-Gani	$15
2498	- BI 2-Gani	$15
2499	- Æ Paika	$15

2500   2501

2500	**Muhammad b. Tughluq (725-752h),** AV Dinar	$1000
2501	- AV Tanka	$600
2502	- AV 'Adli	$800
2503	- AV ½-Dinar	$1500
2504	- AR Tanka	$125

2505   2507

2505	- AR 'Adli	$100
2506	- AR ½-'Adli	*Extremely rare*
2507	- BI Tanka	$30
2508	- BI 10-Gani	$15
2509	- BI 8-Gani	$15
2510	- BI 6-Gani	$15
2511	- BI 2-Gani	$15
2512	- Æ Tanka	$25
2513	- Æ Nisfi (½-Tanka)	$25
2514	- Æ Dirham	$25
2515	- Æ Rab'i (¼-Tanka)	$25
2516	- Æ Paika	$15

2517

| 2517 | **Mahmud b. Muhammad (752h),** AV Tanka | $1200 |

2518   2520   **VF**

2518	**Firuz Shah Tughluq (752-790h),** AV Tanka	$800
2519	- AR Tanka	*Extremely rare*
2520	- BI Tanka	$25
2521	- BI 32-Rati	$15
2522	- Æ Falus	$15
2523	- Æ ½-Falus	$15

2524   2525

2524	**Fath Khan, viceroy (fl.760-761h),** AV Tanka	$1000
2525	- BI Tanka	$30
2526	- BI 32-Rati	$30
2527	**Muhammad b. Firuz, regent (789-790h),** BI Tanka	$50
2528	- Æ Falus	$25

2529

2529	**Tughluq Shah II (790-791h),** AV Tanka	$3000
2530	- BI Tanka	$40
2531	- BI 5/6-Tanka	$25
2532	- BI ½-Tanka	$25
2533	- Æ Falus	$30

2534

| 2534 | **Firuz Shah Zafar (791h),** AV Tanka | $1500 |

		VF
2535	- BI 5/6-Tanka	$30
2536	- BI ½-Tanka	$25
2537	- BI 1/3-Tanka	$25
2538	**Abu Bakr Shah (791-793h),** AV Tanka	$1500
2539	- BI Tanka	$50
2540	- BI 5/6-Tanka	$30
2541	- BI 2/3-Tanka	$30
2542	- BI ½-Tanka	$30
2543	- BI 1/3-Tanka	$25

2544

2544	**Muhammad b. Firuz (792-795h),** AV Tanka	$1500
2545	- BI Tanka	$50
2546	- BI 5/6-Tanka	$25
2547	- BI 1/3-Tanka	$30
2548	- Æ Double Falus	$15
2549	- Æ Falus	$25
2550	- Æ ½-Falus	$25
2551	**Sikandar Shah I (795h),** Æ Double Falus	$40
2552	- Æ Falus	$30
2553	**Mahmud b. Muhammad (795-815h),** AV Tanka	$1500
2554	- AR Tanka	$250
2555	- BI Tanka	$30
2556	- Æ Double Falus	$25
2557	- Æ Falus	$15
2558	**Nusrat Shah (c.797-802h),** AV Tanka	*Extremely rare*
2559	- AR Tanka	*Extremely rare*
2560	- Æ Double Falus	$40
2561	- Æ Falus	$30
2562	*temp.* **Daulat Khan Lodi (815-817h),** AR Tanka	$400
2563	- BI Tanka	$50
2564	*temp.* **Khidr Khan (817-824h),** AR Tanka	$300
2565	- BI Tanka	$40
2566	- Æ Falus	$30
2567	**Mubarak Shah (824-837h),** AV Tanka, in his own name	*Extremely rare*
2568	- AR Tanka, in the name of Muhammad b. Firuz	$300
2569	- AR Tanka, in his own name	$1500
2570	- BI Tanka, in the name of Firuz Shah Tughluq	$25
2571	- Æ Double Falus	$25
2572	- Æ Falus	$25
2573	**Muhammad b. Farid (837-849h),** AV Tanka	$2500
2574	- AR Tanka	$600
2575	- BI Tanka	$30
2576	- BI 32-Rati	$25
2577	- Æ Double Falus	$25

		VF
2578	- Æ Falus	$25
2579	**'Ala al-din 'Alam (849-855h)**, BI Tanka	$150
2580	- Æ Falus	$40
2581	**Bahlul Shah (855-894h)**, BI Tanka	$25
2582	- BI 32-Rati	$15
2583	- Æ Double Falus	$15
2584	- Æ Falus	$10
2585	**Sikandar Shah II (894-923h)**, AV Tanka	*Extremely rare[3]*
2586	- AR Tanka	*Extremely rare[4]*
2587	- BI Tanka	$15
2588	- BI 32-Rati	$15
2589	- BI ¼-Tanka	$25
2590	**Ibrahim Shah (923-932h)**, BI ½-Tanka	$20
2591	- BI ¼-Tanka	$15

2592

2592	**Sher Shah (945-952h)**, AR Rupee	$75
2593	- AR Tanka	$50
2594	- AR ½-Rupee	$300
2595	- Æ Paisa	$15
2596	- Æ ½-Paisa	$25
2597	- Æ 1/8-Paisa	$15
2598	- Æ 1/16-Paisa	$10

2599

2599	**Islam Shah (952-960h)**, AR Rupee	$75
2600	- Æ Paisa	$15
2601	- Æ ½-Paisa	$25
2602	- Æ 1/8-Paisa	$15
2603	**Muhammad 'Adil Shah (960-964h)**, AR Rupee	$60

[3]   Baldwin's Auction 53, 25 September 2007, lot 1614
[4]   Baldwin's Auction 53, 25 September 2007, lot 1615

		VF
2604	- Æ Paisa	$15
2605	- Æ ½-Paisa	$25
2606	**Sikandar Shah III (961-962h)**, AR Rupee	$1000
2607	- Æ Paisa	$125
2608	**Ibrahim Shah (962h)**, AR Rupee	*Extremely rare*[5]
2609	- Æ Paisa	$300
2610	- Æ ½-Paisa	$500

SULTANS OF BENGAL

2611	**Muhammad b. Sam, Ghorid sultan (600-602h)**, AV 20-Rati	$2000
2612	**Rukn al-din 'Ali Mardan (c.606-610h)**, AV 20-Rati	$2000
2613	- AR Tanka	$1000
2614	**Shams al-din Iltutmish of Dehli**, AR Tanka	$200

2615

2615	- AR Tanka, horseman type	$600

2616

2616	**Ghiyath al-din 'Iwad (c.610-624h)**, AR Tanka	$300
2617	**Radiyya of Dehli (634-637h)**, AR Tanka	$750
2618	**Mas'ud of Dehli (639-644h)**, AR Tanka	$750
2619	**Anonymous**, AR Tanka, in the name of the caliph al-Mustansir	$300
2620	**Mahmud of Dehli (644-664h)**, AR Tanka	$150
2621	**Mughith al-din Yuzbak (651-656h)**, AR Tanka	$500

---

[5] Baldwin's Auction 53, 25 September 2007, lot 1620

2622

		VF
2622	**Balban of Dehli (664-686h)**, AR Tanka	$125
2623	**Jalal al-din Mahmud (686h)**, AR Tanka	$400
2624	**Nasir al-din Mahmud (687-688h)**, AR Tanka	$200

2625

2625	**Rukn al-din Kaikaus (689-700h)**, AR Tanka	$125

2626

2626	**Shams al-din Firuz, 1st reign (700-716h)**, AR Tanka	$75
2627	**Shihab al-din Bughda (717-718h)**, AR Tanka	$150
2628	**Shams al-din Firuz, 2nd reign (719-720h)**, AR Tanka	$75

2629

2629	**Ghiyath al-din Bahadur (720-724h)**, AR Tanka	$100
2630	**Nasir al-din Ibrahim (c.724-725h)**, AR Tanka	$1000
2631	**Muhammad b. Tughluq of Dehli**, AV Dinar	$1500

2632

| 2632 | - AR Tanka | $125 |
| 2633 | - Æ Tanka | $30 |

2634

2634   **Fakhr al-din Mubarak (734-750h)**, AR Tanka $60

2635

2635   **'Ala al-din 'Ali (740-746h)**, AR Tanka $125

2636

2636   **Shams al-din Ilyas (743-758h)**, AV Tanka $1500

2637

		VF
2637	- AR Tanka	$80
2638	- AR ¼-Tanka	$300

2639

2639	**Sikandar b. Ilyas (758-792h)**, AV Tanka	$2000

2640

2640	- AR Tanka	$75
2641	**Ghiyath al-din A'zam (792-813h)**, AV Tanka	$2000
2642	- AR Tanka	$60
2643	- AR ¼-Tanka	$150
2644	**Saif al-din Hamza (813-815h)**, AR Tanka	$125

2645

2645	**Shihab al-din Bayazid (815-817h)**, AR Tanka	$125
2646	**'Ala al-din Firuz I (817h)**, AR Tanka	$300
2647	**Jalal al-din Muhammad, 1st reign (818-819h)**, AR Tanka	$100

2648

2648	**Danujamarddana Deva (819-821h),** AR Tanka	$600
2649	**Mahendra Deva (821h),** AR Tanka	$750

2650

2650	**Jalal al-din Muhammad, 2nd reign (821-836h),** AR Tanka	$50
2651	- AR Tanka, *rev.* lion	$1200
2652	**Shams al-din Ahmad (836-837h),** AR Tanka	$250
2653	**Qutb al-din A'zam (c.837h),** AR Tanka	$500
2654	**Nasir al-din Shahim (c.837h),** AR Tanka	*Extremely rare*

2655

2655	**Nasir al-din Mahmud (837-864h),** AV Tanka	$1000
2656	- AR Tanka	$50

2657

2657	- AR Tanka, *obv.* lion	$500
2658	**Rukn al-din Barbak (864-879h),** AR Tanka	$60
2659	**Shams al-din Yusuf (879-885h),** AR Tanka	$75

2660

2660   **Jalal al-din Fath (886-893h)**, AV Tanka $3000

2661

2661	- AR Tanka	$125
2662	**Ghiyath al-din Barbak (893h)**, AV Tanka	*Extremely rare*[6]
2663	- AR Tanka	*Extremely rare*
2664	**Saif al-din Firuz (893-896h)**, AR Tanka	$75
2665	**Qutb al-din Mahmud (896h)**, AR Tanka	$1200

2666

2666	**Shams al-din Muzaffar (896-899h)**, AV Tanka	$5000
2667	- AR Tanka	$150

2668

2668   **'Ala al-din Husain (899-925h)**, AV Tanka $1000

---

6   Baldwin's Auction 89, 8 May 2014, lot 3086

2669

2669	- AR Tanka	**VF** $30

2670

2670	**Nasir al-din Nusrat (925-938h)**, AV Tanka	$1000

2671

2671	- AR Tanka	$30
2672	- AR ½-Tanka	$100
2673	- AR ¼-Tanka	$50

2674

2674	**'Ala al-din Firuz II (938-939h)**, AR Tanka	$100
2675	**Ghiyath al-din Mahmud (939-945h)**, AV Tanka	*Extremely rare*[7]
2676	- AR Tanka	$30
2677	- AR ½-Tanka	$125
2678	- AR ¼-Tanka	$100

---

7   Baldwin's Auction 89, 8 May 2014, lot 3093

2679

VF

2679	**Humayun, Mughal sultan (945h),** AR Rupee	$800
2680	- AR Tanka	$400

2681

2681	**Shams al-din Muhammad Ghazi (960-963h),** AR Rupee	$300
2682	- AR ½-Rupee	$500
2683	**Ghiyath al-din Bahadur (963-968h),** AR Rupee	$50

2684

2684	**Ghiyath al-din Jalal (968-971h),** AR Rupee	$75

2685

2685	**Da'ud Shah (980-984h),** AR Rupee	$125

SULTANS OF MADURA

		VF
2686	**Jalal al-din Ahsan (734-740h)**, AV Tanka	$5000
2687	- AV 1/3-Tanka	*Extremely rare*

2688

2688	- AR 1/3-Tanka	$150
2689	- Æ Paisa	$50
2690	**'Ala al-din Adauji (740h)**, BI Jital	$200
2691	- Æ Paisa	$50
2692	**Qutb al-din Firuz (740h)**, Æ Paisa	$250
2693	**Ghiyath al-din Muhammad Damghan (740-745h)**, AV Tanka	$5000
2694	- AV ½-Tanka	*Extremely rare*
2695	- BI Jital	$75
2696	- Æ Paisa	$40
2697	**Nasir al-din Mahmud Damghan (745-748h)**, BI Jital	$75
2698	- Æ Paisa	$50
2699	**Shams al-din 'Adil (748-760h)**, BI Jital	$75
2700	- Æ Paisa	$30
2701	- Æ ½-Paisa	$25
2702	**Fakhr al-din Mubarak (760-770h)**, BI Jital	$150
2703	- Æ Paisa	$40
2704	- Æ ½-Paisa	$15
2705	**'Ala al-din Sikandar (770-779h)**, Æ Paisa	$60
2706	- Æ ½-Paisa	$30

BAHMANID

2707	**Nasir al-din Isma'il (747-748h)**, BI Jital	$60

2708

2708	**'Ala al-din Bahman (748-760h)**, AR Tanka	$200
2709	- Æ Falus	$15
2710	- Æ ½-Falus	$10
2711	**Muhammad I (760-777h)**, AV Dinar	*Extremely rare*[8]

---

[8]   Baldwin's Auction 53, 25 September 2007, lot 1678

2712

VF

2712   - AV Tanka $1500

2713

2713   - AR Tanka $75
2714   - Æ Falus $15
2715   - Æ ½-Falus $15

2716

2716   **'Ala al-din Mujahid (777-779h)**, AV Tanka   *Extremely rare*
2717   - AR Tanka $400
2718   - Æ Falus $40

2719   2720

2719   **Muhammad II (780-799h)**, AV Tanka $1000
2720   - AR Tanka $50
2721   - Æ Falus $20
2722   **Ghiyath al-din Tahmatan (799h)**, AR Tanka   *Extremely rare*
2723   - Æ Falus $50
2724   **Shams al-din Da'ud II (799-800h)**, AR Tanka   *Extremely rare*[9]

---

9   Baldwin's Auction 53, 25 September 2007, lot 1684

		VF
2725	- Æ Falus	$50
2726	**Taj al-din Firuz (800-825h)**, AV Tanka	*Extremely rare*

2727

2727	- AR Tanka	$50
2728	- Æ Falus	$15

2729

2729	**Shihab al-din Ahmad I (825-838h)**, AR Tanka	$200
2730	- Æ Gani	$40
2731	- Æ ½-Gani	$15
2732	- Æ Falus	$15

2733

2733	**'Ala al-din Ahmad II (838-862h)**, AV Tanka	$800

2734

2734	- AR Tanka	$100
2735	- Æ Gani	$25

		VF
2736	- Æ 2/3-Gani	$25
2737	- Æ ½-Gani	$15
2738	- Æ 1/3-Gani	$15
2739	- Æ 1/6-Gani	$10
2740	**'Ala al-din Humayun (862-866h)**, AV Tanka	$1200
2741	- AR Tanka	$250
2742	- Æ Gani	$40
2743	- Æ 2/3-Gani	$30
2744	- Æ ½-Gani	$25
2745	- Æ 1/3-Gani	$25
2746	**Nizam al-din Ahmad III (866-867h)**, AV Tanka	*Extremely rare*
2747	- Æ Gani	$40
2748	- Æ 2/3-Gani	$30
2749	- Æ ½-Gani	$25
2750	- Æ 1/3-Gani	$25

2751

2751	**Shams al-din Muhammad III (867-887h)**, AV Tanka	$800
2752	- AR Tanka	$100
2753	- Æ Gani	$25
2754	- Æ 2/3-Gani	$25
2755	- Æ ½-Gani	$15
2756	- Æ 1/3-Gani	$15
2757	- Æ 1/6-Gani	$15
2758	**Mahmud Shah (887-924h)**, AV Tanka	$1200
2759	- AR Tanka	$150
2760	- Æ Gani	$25
2761	- Æ 2/3-Gani	$15
2762	- Æ ½-Gani	$15
2763	- Æ 1/3-Gani	$25
2764	- Æ 1/6-Gani	$15
2765	**Wali Allah (929-932h)**, Æ Gani	$30
2766	- Æ 2/3-Gani	$25
2767	- Æ ½-Gani	$25
2768	- Æ 1/3-Gani	$25
2769	**Kalim Allah (932-944h)**, Æ Gani	$30
2770	- Æ 2/3-Gani	$25
2771	- Æ ½-Gani	$25
2772	- Æ 1/3-Gani	$20
2773	- Æ 1/6-Gani	$15

SULTANS OF JAUNPUR

2774

		VF
2774	**Shams al-din Ibrahim (804-844h),** AV Tanka	$1500
2775	- BI Tanka	$25
2776	- BI 32-Rati	$20
2777	- Æ Falus	$15
2778	- Æ ½-Falus	$10

2779

2779	**Nasir al-din Mahmud (844-861h),** AV Tanka	$2000
2780	- BI Tanka	$25
2781	- BI 32-Rati	$20
2782	- Æ Double Falus	$20
2783	- Æ Falus	$15
2784	- Æ ½-Falus	$15
2785	**Muhammad Shah (861-863h),** BI Tanka	$40
2786	- BI 32-Rati	$30
2787	- Æ Double Falus	$25
2788	- Æ Falus	$25

2789

2789	**Husain Shah (863-884h),** AV Tanka	$1500
2790	- BI Tanka	$20
2791	- BI 32-Rati	$25
2792	- Æ Double Falus	$20
2793	- Æ Falus	$15
2794	- Æ ½-Falus	$15
2795	**Barbak Shah (894-896h),** Æ Double Falus	$40
2796	- Æ Falus	$30

SULTANS OF KALPI

		VF
2797	**Fath al-din Jalal (c.837-842h),** Æ Falus	$50

SULTANS OF GUJARAT

2798	**Shams al-din Muzaffar I (810-813h),** AR Tanka	$1500
2799	- Æ Falus	$125
2800	- Æ ½-Falus	$40
2801	**Nasir al-din Ahmad I (813-846h),** AR Tanka	$300
2802	- Æ Falus	$15
2803	- Æ ½-Falus	$10
2804	- Æ ¼-Falus	$10
2805	**Ghiyath al-din Muhammad II (846-855h),** Æ 1½-Falus	$30
2806	- Æ Falus	$15
2807	- Æ ½-Falus	$15
2808	- Æ ¼-Falus	$15
2809	**Qutb al-din Ahmad II (c.855-863h),** AR Tanka	$750
2810	- BI Tanka	$15
2811	- Æ 1½-Falus	$40
2812	- Æ Falus	$15
2813	- Æ ½-Falus	$15

2814

2814	**Nasir al-din Mahmud I (c.863-917h),** AV Tanka	$1000
2815	- AR Tanka	$75

2816

2816	- AR ½-Tanka	$30
2817	- AR ¼-Tanka	$25
2818	- BI Tanka	$25
2819	- Æ 1½-Falus	$20
2820	- Æ Falus	$15
2821	- Æ ½-Falus	$10
2822	- Æ ¼-Falus	$15

2823

		VF
2823	**Shams al-din Muzaffar II (917-932h)**, AV Tanka	$800
2824	- AR Tanka	$50
2825	- AR ½-Tanka	$30
2826	- AR ¼-Tanka	$40
2827	- AR 1/8-Tanka	$30
2828	- AR 1/16-Tanka	$100
2829	- BI Tanka	$25
2830	- BI ½-Tanka	$30
2831	- Æ 2-Falus	$25
2832	- Æ 1½-Falus	$20
2833	- Æ Falus	$15
2834	- Æ ½-Falus	$15
2835	- Æ ¼-Falus	$25
2836	**Nasir al-din Sikandar (932h)**, AV Double Tanka	*Extremely rare*

2837

2837	**Qutb al-din Bahadur (932-943h)**, AV fractional Tanka	$500
2838	- AR Tanka	$75
2839	- AR 1/3-Tanka	$40
2840	- AR 1/6-Tanka	$40
2841	- BI Tanka	$25
2842	- BI ½-Tanka	$20
2843	- Æ 1½-Falus	$20
2844	- Æ Falus	$15
2845	- Æ ½-Falus	$10
2846	**Muhammad Shah III (943-944h)**, AR Tanka	*Extremely rare*

2847

2847	**Nasir al-din Mahmud III (944-961h)**, AV Tanka	$1000
2848	- AR Tanka	$30
2849	- AR ½-Tanka	$25
2850	- AR ¼-Tanka	$25
2851	- BI Tanka	$30
2852	- Æ 1½-Falus	$20

		VF
2853	- Æ Falus	$15
2854	- Æ ½-Falus	$10
2855	- Æ ¼-Falus	$15

2856

2856	**Ghiyath al-din Ahmad III (961-968h),** AV Tanka	$1000
2857	- AR Double Tanka	$125

2858

2858	- AR Tanka	$50
2859	- AR ½-Tanka	$40
2860	- Æ 1½-Falus	$20
2861	- Æ Falus	$15
2862	- Æ ½-Falus	$10

2863   2864

2863	**Shams al-din Muzaffar III, 1ˢᵗ reign (968-980h),** AV Tanka	$1000
2864	- AR Tanka	$40
2865	- AR ½-Tanka	$25
2866	- AR ¼-Tanka	$20
2867	- Æ 1½-Falus	$20
2868	- Æ Falus	$15
2869	- Æ ½-Falus	$15
2870	- Æ ¼-Falus	$15
2871	**Mughal Occupation (980-991h),** AR ½-Tanka, in the name of Akbar	$150

2872

		VF
2872	**Shams al-din Muzaffar III, 2ⁿᵈ reign (991-992h),** AR Rupee	$400

SULTANS OF MALWA

2873	**Hisam al-din Hushang (808-838h),** AV Tanka	$1000

2874

2874	- AR Tanka	$150
2875	- Æ Falus	$15
2876	**Muhammad Shah I (838-839h),** AR Tanka	*Extremely rare*
2877	- Æ Falus	$30
2878	**'Ala al-din Mahmud I (839-873h),** AV Dinar	*Extremely rare[10]*

2879   2881

2879	- AV Tanka	$800
2880	- AR Tanka	$100
2881	- AR ¼-Tanka, posthumous issue	$50
2882	- AR 1/8-Tanka, posthumous issue	$40

¹⁰   Baldwin's Auction 45, 3 May 2006, lot 1291

2883

		VF
2883	- BI Tanka	$50
2884	- BI ½-Tanka	$30
2885	- BI ¼-Tanka	$40
2886	- BI 32-Rati	$40
2887	- Æ 2-Falus	$20
2888	- Æ Falus	$15
2889	- Æ ½-Falus	$20

2890

2890	**Ghiyath Shah, as heir (c.860-873h),** AV Tanka	$1000
2891	- AV ½-Tanka	*Extremely rare*
2892	- AR ½-Tanka	$400
2893	- BI Tanka	$250
2894	- Æ 2-Falus	$30
2895	- Æ Falus	$25
2896	**Ghiyath Shah (873-906h),** AV round Tanka	$1000

2897   2899

2897	- AV square Tanka	$800
2898	- AR Nazarana Tanka (round)	$2500
2899	- AR ½-Tanka	$30
2900	- AR ¼-Tanka	$25
2901	- AR 1/8-Tanka	$25
2902	- Æ 2-Falus	$40
2903	- Æ Falus	$15
2904	- Æ ½-Falus	$10
2905	- Æ 1/3-Falus	$15
2906	- Æ ¼-Falus	$10

2907

2907   **Nasir Shah (906-916h)**, AV Tanka $1000

2908   2909

2908	- AR Tanka	$50
2909	- AR ½-Tanka	$30

2910   2911

2910	- AR ¼-Tanka	$30
2911	- AR 1/8-Tanka	$50
2912	- Æ Falus	$15
2913	- Æ ½-Falus	$10
2914	- Æ ¼-Falus	$10

2915

2915   **Mahmud Shah II (916-937h)**, AV Tanka $1000

2916   2917   2919

2916	- AR Tanka	$50
2917	- AR ½-Tanka	$30
2918	- AR ¼-Tanka	$30
2919	- AR 1/8-Tanka	$50
2920	- Æ Falus	$15
2921	- Æ ½-Falus	$10

		VF
2922	- Æ ¼-Falus	$10
2923	**Muhammad Shah II, pretender (917-922h)**, AR ½-Tanka	$60
2924	- Æ Falus	$25
2925	- Æ ½-Falus	$25
2926	- Æ ¼-Falus	$25
2927	**Ibrahim Shah Lodi of Dehli (c.927-932h)**, AR ½-Tanka	$400
2928	- Æ Falus	$100
2929	**Rana Sangram of Mewar (fl.931h)**, AR ½-Tanka	$250
2930	- Æ Falus	$100
2931	**Bahadur Shah of Gujarat (937-943h)**, Æ 1½-Falus	$15
2932	- Æ Falus	$15
2933	**Mahmud III of Gujarat (944-949h)**, Æ Falus	$15
2934	- Æ ½-Falus	$15
2935	**Muhammad b. Muzaffar (962-964h)**, AR Tanka	$100
2936	- Æ Falus	$25
2937	- Æ ½-Falus	$15

2938

2938	**Baz Bahadur (963-969h)**, AR Tanka	$75
2939	- Æ Falus	$15
2940	- Æ ½-Falus	$15

SULTANS OF KASHMIR

2941

2941	*temp.* **Sikandar Shah I (c.796-816h)**, Æ Falus	$125
2942	**Zain al-'Abidin (823-874h)**, AV Dinar	*Extremely rare[11]*
2943	- AR Tanka	$800
2944	- AR Sasnu	$50
2945	- Æ Kaserah	$15
2946	- Æ ½-Kaserah	$20

---

[11]   Baldwin's Auction 50, 24 April 2007, lot 934

2947

		VF
2947	**Haidar Shah (874-876h),** AR Sasnu	$75
2948	- Æ Kaserah	$25
2949	- Æ ½-Kaserah	$30
2950	**Hasan Shah (876-889h),** AV Dinar	Extremely rare[12]
2951	- AR Sasnu	$50
2952	- Æ Kaserah	$15
2953	- Æ ½-Kaserah	$25
2954	**Muhammad Shah (c.889-892, 904-910, 920-921, 923-934, 937-943h),** AV Dinar	Extremely rare[13]
2955	- AR Sasnu	$50
2956	- Æ Kaserah	$15
2957	- Æ ½-Kaserah	$25
2958	**Fath Shah (892-904, 910-920, 921-923h),** AV Dinar	$2500

2959

2959	- AR Sasnu	$50
2960	- Æ Kaserah	$15
2961	- Æ ½-Kaserah	$40
2962	**Sikandar Shah (c.923h),** AV Dinar	Extremely rare[14]
2963	- AR Sasnu	$75
2964	- Æ Kaserah	$25
2965	**Ibrahim Shah (c.934-936h),** AR Sasnu	$50
2966	- Æ Kaserah	$15
2967	**Sa'id Khan of Kashghar (939-940h),** AR Sasnu	$75
2968	- Æ Kaserah	$25
2969	**Shams al-din II (c.943-945h),** AR Sasnu	$75
2970	**Isma'il Shah I (c.945-947h),** AR Sasnu	$75
2971	- Æ Kaserah	$25
2972	**Nazuk Shah, 2nd reign (947-953h),** AR Sasnu, in the name of Nadir	$75
2973	- Æ Kaserah	$25

[12]   The New York Sale XXV, 5 January 2011, lot 365
[13]   Baldwin's Auction 89, 8 May 2014, lot 3158
[14]   Baldwin's Auction 89, 8 May 2014, lot 3159

	2974	**VF**
2974	*temp*. **Haidar Dughlat (953-957h)**, AR Sasnu, in the name of Humayun	$60
2975	**Nazuk Shah, 3rd reign (957-958h)**, AR Sasnu, in the name of Nadir	$50
2976	**Isma'il Shah II (961-962h)**, AR Sasnu	$150

2977

2977	**Habib Shah (962h)**, AR Sasnu, in the name of Mahmud	$125
2978	**Muhammad Ghazi Shah (962-970h)**, AR Sasnu	$75
2979	**Husain Shah (970-979h)**, AR Sasnu	$50
2980	- Æ Kaserah	$15
2981	**Muhammad 'Ali Shah (978-987h)**, AR Sasnu	$50

2982

2982	**Muhammad Yusuf Shah (987, 988-994h)**, AR Sasnu	$50
2983	- Æ Kaserah	$15
2984	**Akbar,** AR Sasnu	$60
2985	- Æ Kaserah	$25

SOUTH-EAST ASIA

Malaya and Indonesia were an important part of the trade route between India and China and were regularly visited by Arab traders. Eventually, several small Islamic kingdoms were established. The earliest of these was the sultanate of Samudra-Pasai, founded in the 7th century AH in northern Sumatra. The later sultanates of this region fall outside the scope of the present volume.

SAMUDRA-PASAI

Leyten, J., *Gold coins of Samudra-Pasai and Acheh: Their origin, name and weight in a historical context*, Amsterdam, 2004

		VF
2986	**Munawar (c.668h),** AV ½-Kupang	$100

2987

2987	**Ahmad I (c.668-694h),** AV Kupang	$75
2988	- AV ½-Kupang	$75

2989

2989	**Salah al-din (c.689-696h),** AV Kupang	$100

2990

2990	**Muhammad (c.696-726h),** AV Kupang	$60

2991

2991	**Mansur (c.696-733h),** AV Kupang	$100
2992	**Ahmad II (c.726-761h),** AV Kupang	$60

2993

2993	**Zain al-'Abidin I (c.761-771h),** AV Kupang	$100
2994	**Ala'lilah (c.771-781h),** AV Kupang	$75

2995

	VF
2995	**'Abd Allah I (c.781-802h)**, AV Kupang	$60
2996	**Abu'l-din (c.808-815h)**, AV Kupang	$75

2997

2997	**'Addallah (c.815-838h)**, AV Kupang	$60
2998	**Ahmad III (c.838-856h)**, AV Kupang	$60
2999	**'Abd Allah II (c.880-919h)**, AV Kupang	$60

APPENDIX I

These are some of the most commonly encountered Islamic mints:

'Adan (Aden)	عدن	Laknauti	لكنوتى
Amul	امل	Madinat al-Salam (Baghdad)	
al-Andalus (Spain)	الاندلس		مدينة السلام
Ardabil	اردبيل	Mardin	ماردين
Arminiya (Armenia)	ارمينيه	Marw	مرو
Arrajan	ارجان	al-Mawsil (Mosul)	الموصل
Astarabad	استراباد	Misr (Egypt)	مصر
Isbahan/Isfahan	اصفهان/اصبهان	al-Muhammadiya	المحمدية
Balkh	بلخ	Nasibin	نصيبين
al-Basra	البصرة	Nishapur	نيشابور
Bukhara	بخارا	al-Qahira (Cairo)	القاهرة
Dehli	دهلى	Qazvin	قزوين
Dimashq (Damascus)	دمشق	Qumm	قم
Fas (Fez)	فاس	Quniya (Konya)	قونية
Filastin (Palestine)	فلسطين	Samarqand	سمرقند
Firuzabad	فيروزاباد	San'a	صنعا
Ghazna	غزنة	al-Shash (Tashkent)	الشاش
Halab (Aleppo)	حلب	Shiraz	شيراز
Hamadan	همدان	Sijistan	سجستان
Herat	هراة	Sivas	سيواس
Jurjan	جرجان	Tabriz	تبريز
Kashan	كاشان	Wasit	واسط
Khwarizm	خوارزم	Yazd	يزد
Kirman	كرمان	Zabid	زبيد
al-Kufa	الكوفة		

APPENDIX II

Arabic numbers

(most coins of the period covered by this volume
have dates written in words rather than numerals)

ahd	1	احد	‘ashrin	20	عشرين
ithnatayn	2	اثنتين	thalathin	30	ثلثين
thulth	3	ثلث	arba‘in	40	اربعين
arba’	4	اربع	khamsin	50	خمسين
khams	5	خمس	sittin	60	ستين
sitt	6	ست	seb‘in	70	سبعين
seb’	7	سبع	themanin	80	ثمانين
theman	8	ثمان	tis‘in	90	تسعين
tis’	9	تسع	mi’a	100	مائة
‘ashra	10	عشرة	mi’atin	200	مائتين

Examples:

132 = اثنتين و ثلثين و مائة

247 = سبع و اربعين و مائتين

365 = خمس و ستين و ثلثمائة

APPENDIX III

Abbasid Caliphs:

al-Saffah (132-136h)	السفاح
al-Mansur (136-158h)	المنصور
al-Mahdi (158-169h)	المهدى
al-Hadi (169-170h)	الهادى
al-Rashid (170-193h)	الرشيد
al-Amin (193-198h)	الامين
al-Ma'mun (194-218h)	المأمون
al-Mu'tasim (218-227h)	المعتصم
al-Wathiq (227-232h)	الواثق
al-Mutawakkil (232-247h)	المتوكل
al-Muntasir (247-248h)	المنتصر
al-Musta'in (248-251h)	المستعين
al-Mu'tazz (251-255h)	المعتز
al-Muhtadi (255-256h)	المهتدى
al-Mu'tamid (256-279h)	المعتمد
al-Mu'tadid (279-289h)	المعتضد
al-Muktafi (289-295h)	المكتفى
al-Muqtadir (295-320h)	المقتدر
al-Qahir (320-322h)	القاهر
al-Radi (322-329h)	الراضى
al-Muttaqi (329-333h)	المتقى
al-Mustakfi (333-334h)	المستكفى

al-Muti' (334-363h)	المطيع
al-Ta'i' (363-381h)	الطائع
al-Qadir (381-422h)	القادر
al-Qa'im (422-467h)	القائم
al-Muqtadi (467-487h)	المقتدى
al-Mustazhir (487-512h)	المستظهر
al-Mustarshid (512-529h)	المسترشد
al-Muqtafi (530-555h)	المقتفى
al-Mustanjid (555-556h)	المستنجد
al-Mustadi (566-575h)	المستضى
al-Nasir (575-622h)	الناصر
al-Zahir (622-623h)	الظاهر
al-Mustansir (623-640h)	المستنصر
al-Musta'sim (640-656h)	المستعصم

APPENDIX IV

These are some of the most commonly encountered names of Islamic rulers:

'Abd al-'Aziz	عبد العزيز	Nasr	ناصر
'Abd Allah	عبد الله	Sa'id	سعيد
'Abd al-Malik	عبد الملك	Sulayman	سليمان
'Abd al-Rahman	عبد الرحمن	Tahir	طاهر
Abu Bakr	ابو بكر	Timur	تيمور
Ahmad	احمد	Tughril	طغرل
'Ali	علی	'Umar	عمر
Arslan	ارسلان	'Uthman	عثمان
Ashraf	اشرف	Yahya	يحيى
Da'ud	دأود	Ya'qub	يعقوب
Firuz	فيروز	Yusuf	يوسف
Harun	هرون		
Hasan	حسن		
Husayn	حسين		
Ibrahim	ابراهيم		
Ishaq	اشحاق		
Isma'il	اسمعيل		
Ja'far	جعفر		
Khalid	خلد		
Khusraw	خسرو		
Mahmud	محمود		
Mansur	منصور		
Mas'ud	مسعود		
Muhammad	محمد		
Musa	موسى		

APPENDIX V

IMAGE CREDITS:

1	Wilkes & Curtis Ltd
2	Ashmolean Museum, Oxford
4	Ashmolean Museum, Oxford
5	Wilkes & Curtis Ltd
7	Wilkes & Curtis Ltd
8	Wilkes & Curtis Ltd
9	Ashmolean Museum, Oxford
10	Morton & Eden Ltd
11	Ashmolean Museum, Oxford
12	Wilkes & Curtis Ltd
13	Ashmolean Museum, Oxford
14	Wilkes & Curtis Ltd
15	Ashmolean Museum, Oxford
16	Wilkes & Curtis Ltd
18	Wilkes & Curtis Ltd
19	Ashmolean Museum, Oxford
22	Wilkes & Curtis Ltd
23	Wilkes & Curtis Ltd
24	Wilkes & Curtis Ltd
27	Wilkes & Curtis Ltd
28	Ashmolean Museum, Oxford
29	Ashmolean Museum, Oxford
32	Wilkes & Curtis Ltd
34	A. H. Baldwin & Sons Ltd
36	Ashmolean Museum, Oxford
37	Classical Numismatic Group, Inc.
38	Wilkes & Curtis Ltd
39	Ashmolean Museum, Oxford
41	Wilkes & Curtis Ltd
42	Ashmolean Museum, Oxford
44	Wilkes & Curtis Ltd
50	Wilkes & Curtis Ltd
52	Wilkes & Curtis Ltd
54	Wilkes & Curtis Ltd
55	Wilkes & Curtis Ltd
58	Ashmolean Museum, Oxford
62	Ashmolean Museum, Oxford
68	Morton & Eden Ltd
71	Wilkes & Curtis Ltd
74	Classical Numismatic Group, Inc.
75	A. H. Baldwin & Sons Ltd
78	Morton & Eden Ltd
79	Wilkes & Curtis Ltd
83	Morton & Eden Ltd
89	Morton & Eden Ltd
90	Morton & Eden Ltd
93	Ashmolean Museum, Oxford
96	Ashmolean Museum, Oxford
101	A. H. Baldwin & Sons Ltd
103	Ashmolean Museum, Oxford
104	Ashmolean Museum, Oxford
105	A. H. Baldwin & Sons Ltd
107	Ashmolean Museum, Oxford
111	Ashmolean Museum, Oxford
112	Ashmolean Museum, Oxford
115	Ashmolean Museum, Oxford
117	Ashmolean Museum, Oxford
118	Ashmolean Museum, Oxford
120	Ashmolean Museum, Oxford
121	Morton & Eden Ltd
123	Ashmolean Museum, Oxford
126	Ashmolean Museum, Oxford
127	Ashmolean Museum, Oxford
128	Wilkes & Curtis Ltd
131	Ashmolean Museum, Oxford
132	Wilkes & Curtis Ltd
133	Ashmolean Museum, Oxford
134	Ashmolean Museum, Oxford
136	Ashmolean Museum, Oxford
138	Ashmolean Museum, Oxford
139	Ashmolean Museum, Oxford
142	Morton & Eden Ltd
143	A. H. Baldwin & Sons Ltd
148	Ashmolean Museum, Oxford
149	Morton & Eden Ltd
152	Ashmolean Museum, Oxford
154	A. H. Baldwin & Sons Ltd
155	Morton & Eden Ltd
161	Ashmolean Museum, Oxford
178	Ashmolean Museum, Oxford
189	Ashmolean Museum, Oxford
201	Wilkes & Curtis Ltd
226	Ashmolean Museum, Oxford
227	Morton & Eden Ltd
228	A. H. Baldwin & Sons Ltd
231	Morton & Eden Ltd
232	Morton & Eden Ltd
237	Ashmolean Museum, Oxford
238	Wilkes & Curtis Ltd
241	Ashmolean Museum, Oxford
245	Ashmolean Museum, Oxford
252	Ashmolean Museum, Oxford
258	Wilkes & Curtis Ltd
262	Ashmolean Museum, Oxford
266	Ashmolean Museum, Oxford
268	Ashmolean Museum, Oxford
275	Ashmolean Museum, Oxford
280	Ashmolean Museum, Oxford

281	Ashmolean Museum, Oxford		435	Morton & Eden Ltd
297	Ashmolean Museum, Oxford		436	Ashmolean Museum, Oxford
299	Morton & Eden Ltd		437	Wilkes & Curtis Ltd
314	Ashmolean Museum, Oxford		438	Morton & Eden Ltd
329	Ashmolean Museum, Oxford		439	Wilkes & Curtis Ltd
337	Wilkes & Curtis Ltd		440	Ashmolean Museum, Oxford
343	Wilkes & Curtis Ltd		441	Wilkes & Curtis Ltd
345	Ashmolean Museum, Oxford		442	Morton & Eden Ltd
356	Ashmolean Museum, Oxford		443	A. H. Baldwin & Sons Ltd
362	Wilkes & Curtis Ltd		444	Ashmolean Museum, Oxford
366	Ashmolean Museum, Oxford		446	Ashmolean Museum, Oxford
367	Ashmolean Museum, Oxford		449	Wilkes & Curtis Ltd
369	Morton & Eden Ltd		450	Morton & Eden Ltd
371	Ashmolean Museum, Oxford		451	A. H. Baldwin & Sons Ltd
374	Ashmolean Museum, Oxford		452	Ashmolean Museum, Oxford
375	Ashmolean Museum, Oxford		453	Ashmolean Museum, Oxford
376	Ashmolean Museum, Oxford		455	Morton & Eden Ltd
377	Ashmolean Museum, Oxford		456	Morton & Eden Ltd
378	Ashmolean Museum, Oxford		457	Ashmolean Museum, Oxford
379	Ashmolean Museum, Oxford		459	A. H. Baldwin & Sons Ltd
381	Ashmolean Museum, Oxford		460	Morton & Eden Ltd
382	Wilkes & Curtis Ltd		462	Wilkes & Curtis Ltd
384	Ashmolean Museum, Oxford		463	Wilkes & Curtis Ltd
386	Ashmolean Museum, Oxford		469	Ashmolean Museum, Oxford
387	Ashmolean Museum, Oxford		470	Wilkes & Curtis Ltd
389	Wilkes & Curtis Ltd		471	Ashmolean Museum, Oxford
390	Ashmolean Museum, Oxford		472	Ashmolean Museum, Oxford
391	Ashmolean Museum, Oxford		474	Ashmolean Museum, Oxford
394	Wilkes & Curtis Ltd		475	Ashmolean Museum, Oxford
397	Wilkes & Curtis Ltd		476	Ashmolean Museum, Oxford
398	Ashmolean Museum, Oxford		477	Ashmolean Museum, Oxford
399	Ashmolean Museum, Oxford		489	Wilkes & Curtis Ltd
400	Ashmolean Museum, Oxford		495	Ashmolean Museum, Oxford
401	Ashmolean Museum, Oxford		500	Wilkes & Curtis Ltd
404	Ashmolean Museum, Oxford		526	Ashmolean Museum, Oxford
405	Wilkes & Curtis Ltd		533	Ashmolean Museum, Oxford
409	Ashmolean Museum, Oxford		534	Wilkes & Curtis Ltd
410	Wilkes & Curtis Ltd		546	Ashmolean Museum, Oxford
411	Ashmolean Museum, Oxford		547	Wilkes & Curtis Ltd
412	Wilkes & Curtis Ltd		548	Ashmolean Museum, Oxford
413	Ashmolean Museum, Oxford		549	Ashmolean Museum, Oxford
416	Wilkes & Curtis Ltd		550	Ashmolean Museum, Oxford
417	Wilkes & Curtis Ltd		554	Morton & Eden Ltd
418	A. H. Baldwin & Sons Ltd		556	Ashmolean Museum, Oxford
420	Wilkes & Curtis Ltd		557	Morton & Eden Ltd
422	Ashmolean Museum, Oxford		558	Ashmolean Museum, Oxford
423	Ashmolean Museum, Oxford		560	Ashmolean Museum, Oxford
425	Wilkes & Curtis Ltd		562	Ashmolean Museum, Oxford
426	Ashmolean Museum, Oxford		563	Morton & Eden Ltd
427	Wilkes & Curtis Ltd		564	Ashmolean Museum, Oxford
428	Morton & Eden Ltd		565	Morton & Eden Ltd
429	Wilkes & Curtis Ltd		566	Ashmolean Museum, Oxford
431	Ashmolean Museum, Oxford		567	A. H. Baldwin & Sons Ltd
432	Wilkes & Curtis Ltd		575	Ashmolean Museum, Oxford
433	Ashmolean Museum, Oxford		577	Ashmolean Museum, Oxford

578	Ashmolean Museum, Oxford
579	Ashmolean Museum, Oxford
581	Ashmolean Museum, Oxford
582	Dix Noonan Webb Ltd
585	Ashmolean Museum, Oxford
586	Ashmolean Museum, Oxford
595	Ashmolean Museum, Oxford
598	Ashmolean Museum, Oxford
599	Ashmolean Museum, Oxford
604	Ashmolean Museum, Oxford
607	Ashmolean Museum, Oxford
610	Ashmolean Museum, Oxford
617	Ashmolean Museum, Oxford
618	Ashmolean Museum, Oxford
620	Ashmolean Museum, Oxford
621	Ashmolean Museum, Oxford
623	Ashmolean Museum, Oxford
629	Morton & Eden Ltd
630	Morton & Eden Ltd
634	Morton & Eden Ltd
636	A. H. Baldwin & Sons Ltd
637	Ashmolean Museum, Oxford
639	Ashmolean Museum, Oxford
640	Ashmolean Museum, Oxford
641	Ashmolean Museum, Oxford
642	Ashmolean Museum, Oxford
643	Wilkes & Curtis Ltd
645	Ashmolean Museum, Oxford
647	Ashmolean Museum, Oxford
649	Ashmolean Museum, Oxford
650	Wilkes & Curtis Ltd
651	Ashmolean Museum, Oxford
653	Morton & Eden Ltd
654	Ashmolean Museum, Oxford
655	Ashmolean Museum, Oxford
658	Wilkes & Curtis Ltd
661	Ashmolean Museum, Oxford
662	Ashmolean Museum, Oxford
665	Ashmolean Museum, Oxford
667	Ashmolean Museum, Oxford
668	Ashmolean Museum, Oxford
669	Ashmolean Museum, Oxford
670	Ashmolean Museum, Oxford
672	Ashmolean Museum, Oxford
673	Ashmolean Museum, Oxford
675	Wilkes & Curtis Ltd
676	Wilkes & Curtis Ltd
681	Ashmolean Museum, Oxford
685	Ashmolean Museum, Oxford
686	Wilkes & Curtis Ltd
687	Ashmolean Museum, Oxford
689	Ashmolean Museum, Oxford
690	Ashmolean Museum, Oxford
692	Ashmolean Museum, Oxford
694	Ashmolean Museum, Oxford
695	Ashmolean Museum, Oxford
697	Ashmolean Museum, Oxford
698	Wilkes & Curtis Ltd
700	Wilkes & Curtis Ltd
702	Ashmolean Museum, Oxford
703	Ashmolean Museum, Oxford
704	Wilkes & Curtis Ltd
705	A. H. Baldwin & Sons Ltd
711	Morton & Eden Ltd
715	Ashmolean Museum, Oxford
716	Ashmolean Museum, Oxford
717	Spink & Son Ltd
718	Wilkes & Curtis Ltd
720	Morton & Eden Ltd
721	Spink & Son Ltd
727	A. H. Baldwin & Sons Ltd
734	Wilkes & Curtis Ltd
736	Wilkes & Curtis Ltd
737	Wilkes & Curtis Ltd
741	Ashmolean Museum, Oxford
746	Wilkes & Curtis Ltd
747	Wilkes & Curtis Ltd
753	Wilkes & Curtis Ltd
756	Wilkes & Curtis Ltd
758	Wilkes & Curtis Ltd
763	A. H. Baldwin & Sons Ltd
779	Wilkes & Curtis Ltd
781	Ashmolean Museum, Oxford
782	Ashmolean Museum, Oxford
784	Morton & Eden Ltd
786	Wilkes & Curtis Ltd
789	Ashmolean Museum, Oxford
790	Ashmolean Museum, Oxford
792	Wilkes & Curtis Ltd
793	Ashmolean Museum, Oxford
794	Ashmolean Museum, Oxford
796	Wilkes & Curtis Ltd
799	Classical Numismatic Group, Inc.
803	Ashmolean Museum, Oxford
805	Ashmolean Museum, Oxford
807	Ashmolean Museum, Oxford
808	Ashmolean Museum, Oxford
809	Ashmolean Museum, Oxford
811	Ashmolean Museum, Oxford
814	Ashmolean Museum, Oxford
815	Morton & Eden Ltd
816	Ashmolean Museum, Oxford
819	Wilkes & Curtis Ltd
820	Wilkes & Curtis Ltd
822	Ashmolean Museum, Oxford
823	Ashmolean Museum, Oxford
825	Ashmolean Museum, Oxford
826	Ashmolean Museum, Oxford
827	Wilkes & Curtis Ltd
829	Ashmolean Museum, Oxford

831	Wilkes & Curtis Ltd	960	Ashmolean Museum, Oxford
833	Morton & Eden Ltd	963	Morton & Eden Ltd
835	Spink & Son Ltd	966	Morton & Eden Ltd
836	Wilkes & Curtis Ltd	967	Ashmolean Museum, Oxford
837	Ashmolean Museum, Oxford	974	Wilkes & Curtis Ltd
838	Ashmolean Museum, Oxford	980	Morton & Eden Ltd
839	Wilkes & Curtis Ltd	981	Ashmolean Museum, Oxford
842	Morton & Eden Ltd	985	Morton & Eden Ltd
843	Wilkes & Curtis Ltd	990	Ashmolean Museum, Oxford
846	Ashmolean Museum, Oxford	996	Wilkes & Curtis Ltd
850	Ashmolean Museum, Oxford	998	Ashmolean Museum, Oxford
851	Ashmolean Museum, Oxford	999	Ashmolean Museum, Oxford
852	Wilkes & Curtis Ltd	1001	Wilkes & Curtis Ltd
853	Morton & Eden Ltd	1004	Morton & Eden Ltd
854	Morton & Eden Ltd	1007	Morton & Eden Ltd
856	Wilkes & Curtis Ltd	1009	Ashmolean Museum, Oxford
860	Wilkes & Curtis Ltd	1010	Morton & Eden Ltd
861	Ashmolean Museum, Oxford	1012	Ashmolean Museum, Oxford
865	Ashmolean Museum, Oxford	1013	Ashmolean Museum, Oxford
867	Wilkes & Curtis Ltd	1017	Morton & Eden Ltd
869	Ashmolean Museum, Oxford	1023	Wilkes & Curtis Ltd
872	Wilkes & Curtis Ltd	1025	Ashmolean Museum, Oxford
873	Wilkes & Curtis Ltd	1029	Morton & Eden Ltd
874	Morton & Eden Ltd	1030	Morton & Eden Ltd
875	Morton & Eden Ltd	1032	Ashmolean Museum, Oxford
882	A. H. Baldwin & Sons Ltd	1033	Morton & Eden Ltd
887	Wilkes & Curtis Ltd	1034	Wilkes & Curtis Ltd
888	Ashmolean Museum, Oxford	1040	Ashmolean Museum, Oxford
889	Spink & Son Ltd	1045	Morton & Eden Ltd
890	Wilkes & Curtis Ltd	1046	Ashmolean Museum, Oxford
891	Wilkes & Curtis Ltd	1047	Ashmolean Museum, Oxford
892	Wilkes & Curtis Ltd	1049	Morton & Eden Ltd
896	Classical Numismatic Group, Inc.	1050	Ashmolean Museum, Oxford
898	Ashmolean Museum, Oxford	1051	Ashmolean Museum, Oxford
899	Ashmolean Museum, Oxford	1052	Wilkes & Curtis Ltd
904	Ashmolean Museum, Oxford	1057	Ashmolean Museum, Oxford
906	Ashmolean Museum, Oxford	1058	Ashmolean Museum, Oxford
910	Wilkes & Curtis Ltd	1062	Ashmolean Museum, Oxford
911	Ashmolean Museum, Oxford	1068	Ashmolean Museum, Oxford
914	Ashmolean Museum, Oxford	1072	Ashmolean Museum, Oxford
915	Wilkes & Curtis Ltd	1075	Ashmolean Museum, Oxford
916	Ashmolean Museum, Oxford	1077	A. H. Baldwin & Sons Ltd
918	Ashmolean Museum, Oxford	1078	Ashmolean Museum, Oxford
919	Wilkes & Curtis Ltd	1083	Ashmolean Museum, Oxford
925	Ashmolean Museum, Oxford	1084	Wilkes & Curtis Ltd
926	Ashmolean Museum, Oxford	1089	Morton & Eden Ltd
927	Ashmolean Museum, Oxford	1093	Ashmolean Museum, Oxford
928	Wilkes & Curtis Ltd	1095	Wilkes & Curtis Ltd
931	Ashmolean Museum, Oxford	1098	Spink & Son Ltd
941	Wilkes & Curtis Ltd	1099	Wilkes & Curtis Ltd
953	Wilkes & Curtis Ltd	1100	Wilkes & Curtis Ltd
954	Ashmolean Museum, Oxford	1103	A. H. Baldwin & Sons Ltd
955	Morton & Eden Ltd	1104	Ashmolean Museum, Oxford
957	Wilkes & Curtis Ltd	1106	Ashmolean Museum, Oxford
959	Wilkes & Curtis Ltd	1107	Wilkes & Curtis Ltd

1108	Ashmolean Museum, Oxford
1109	Wilkes & Curtis Ltd
1111	Wilkes & Curtis Ltd
1113	Wilkes & Curtis Ltd
1115	Wilkes & Curtis Ltd
1121	Ashmolean Museum, Oxford
1124	Wilkes & Curtis Ltd
1127	Wilkes & Curtis Ltd
1129	Ashmolean Museum, Oxford
1130	Ashmolean Museum, Oxford
1131	Ashmolean Museum, Oxford
1132	Wilkes & Curtis Ltd
1135	Wilkes & Curtis Ltd
1137	Wilkes & Curtis Ltd
1138	Ashmolean Museum, Oxford
1139	Wilkes & Curtis Ltd
1144	Wilkes & Curtis Ltd
1148	Morton & Eden Ltd
1149	Wilkes & Curtis Ltd
1151	Ashmolean Museum, Oxford
1152	Morton & Eden Ltd
1156	A. H. Baldwin & Sons Ltd
1157	A. H. Baldwin & Sons Ltd
1158	Ashmolean Museum, Oxford
1174	Classical Numismatic Group, Inc.
1175	Classical Numismatic Group, Inc.
1176	Ashmolean Museum, Oxford
1177	Classical Numismatic Group, Inc.
1178	Classical Numismatic Group, Inc.
1179	Classical Numismatic Group, Inc.
1180	Classical Numismatic Group, Inc.
1181	Wilkes & Curtis Ltd
1182	Wilkes & Curtis Ltd
1183	Classical Numismatic Group, Inc.
1184	Classical Numismatic Group, Inc.
1185	Classical Numismatic Group, Inc.
1186	Classical Numismatic Group, Inc.
1187	Classical Numismatic Group, Inc.
1188	Classical Numismatic Group, Inc.
1190	Wilkes & Curtis Ltd
1191	Classical Numismatic Group, Inc.
1193	Wilkes & Curtis Ltd
1195	Classical Numismatic Group, Inc.
1198	Classical Numismatic Group, Inc.
1199	Classical Numismatic Group, Inc.
1200	Classical Numismatic Group, Inc.
1201	Classical Numismatic Group, Inc.
1202	Classical Numismatic Group, Inc.
1203	Wilkes & Curtis Ltd
1204	Ashmolean Museum, Oxford
1205	Wilkes & Curtis Ltd
1206	Wilkes & Curtis Ltd
1207	Classical Numismatic Group, Inc.
1208	Classical Numismatic Group, Inc.
1209	Ashmolean Museum, Oxford
1210	Ashmolean Museum, Oxford
1211	Classical Numismatic Group, Inc.
1212	Wilkes & Curtis Ltd
1213	Classical Numismatic Group, Inc.
1214	Wilkes & Curtis Ltd
1217	Ashmolean Museum, Oxford
1219	Ashmolean Museum, Oxford
1220	Ashmolean Museum, Oxford
1221	Classical Numismatic Group, Inc.
1222	Classical Numismatic Group, Inc.
1223	Ashmolean Museum, Oxford
1224	Ashmolean Museum, Oxford
1239	Wilkes & Curtis Ltd
1240	Ashmolean Museum, Oxford
1242	Ashmolean Museum, Oxford
1243	Classical Numismatic Group, Inc.
1244	Ashmolean Museum, Oxford
1245	Classical Numismatic Group, Inc.
1246	Classical Numismatic Group, Inc.
1248	Classical Numismatic Group, Inc.
1250	Classical Numismatic Group, Inc.
1252	Morton & Eden Ltd
1253	Classical Numismatic Group, Inc.
1254	Wilkes & Curtis Ltd
1255	Wilkes & Curtis Ltd
1256	Wilkes & Curtis Ltd
1258	Wilkes & Curtis Ltd
1259	Classical Numismatic Group, Inc.
1263	Wilkes & Curtis Ltd
1265	Classical Numismatic Group, Inc.
1266	Ashmolean Museum, Oxford
1267	Wilkes & Curtis Ltd
1268	Wilkes & Curtis Ltd
1269	Ashmolean Museum, Oxford
1270	Classical Numismatic Group, Inc.
1271	Wilkes & Curtis Ltd
1272	Classical Numismatic Group, Inc.
1273	Classical Numismatic Group, Inc.
1275	Ashmolean Museum, Oxford
1276	Classical Numismatic Group, Inc.
1278	Classical Numismatic Group, Inc.
1279	Ashmolean Museum, Oxford
1281	Ashmolean Museum, Oxford
1283	Ashmolean Museum, Oxford
1286	Wilkes & Curtis Ltd
1289	Ashmolean Museum, Oxford
1290	Ashmolean Museum, Oxford
1295	Ashmolean Museum, Oxford
1300	Ashmolean Museum, Oxford
1302	Ashmolean Museum, Oxford
1305	Classical Numismatic Group, Inc.
1307	Spink & Son Ltd
1308	Ashmolean Museum, Oxford
1318	Ashmolean Museum, Oxford
1319	Ashmolean Museum, Oxford

1324	Wilkes & Curtis Ltd
1326	Ashmolean Museum, Oxford
1327	Ashmolean Museum, Oxford
1328	Ashmolean Museum, Oxford
1330	Ashmolean Museum, Oxford
1332	Ashmolean Museum, Oxford
1333	Morton & Eden Ltd
1334	Ashmolean Museum, Oxford
1335	Wilkes & Curtis Ltd
1337	Morton & Eden Ltd
1339	Ashmolean Museum, Oxford
1340	Ashmolean Museum, Oxford
1341	Wilkes & Curtis Ltd
1343	Morton & Eden Ltd
1344	Ashmolean Museum, Oxford
1347	Ashmolean Museum, Oxford
1348	Morton & Eden Ltd
1349	Ashmolean Museum, Oxford
1350	Wilkes & Curtis Ltd
1353	Ashmolean Museum, Oxford
1355	Morton & Eden Ltd
1356	Wilkes & Curtis Ltd
1359	Ashmolean Museum, Oxford
1365	Ashmolean Museum, Oxford
1366	Ashmolean Museum, Oxford
1372	Ashmolean Museum, Oxford
1389	Ashmolean Museum, Oxford
1394	Ashmolean Museum, Oxford
1397	Ashmolean Museum, Oxford
1402	Ashmolean Museum, Oxford
1408	Wilkes & Curtis Ltd
1412	Ashmolean Museum, Oxford
1415	Wilkes & Curtis Ltd
1416	Wilkes & Curtis Ltd
1417	Ashmolean Museum, Oxford
1418	Wilkes & Curtis Ltd
1421	Wilkes & Curtis Ltd
1424	A. H. Baldwin & Sons Ltd
1425	Morton & Eden Ltd
1429	Wilkes & Curtis Ltd
1430	Wilkes & Curtis Ltd
1434	Ashmolean Museum, Oxford
1435	A. H. Baldwin & Sons Ltd
1439	Wilkes & Curtis Ltd
1440	Ashmolean Museum, Oxford
1442	Wilkes & Curtis Ltd
1443	A. H. Baldwin & Sons Ltd
1444	Ashmolean Museum, Oxford
1445	Wilkes & Curtis Ltd
1449	Wilkes & Curtis Ltd
1451	Wilkes & Curtis Ltd
1454	Wilkes & Curtis Ltd
1455	Wilkes & Curtis Ltd
1460	Wilkes & Curtis Ltd
1461	Wilkes & Curtis Ltd
1462	Wilkes & Curtis Ltd
1464	Morton & Eden Ltd
1469	Wilkes & Curtis Ltd
1471	Ashmolean Museum, Oxford
1473	A. H. Baldwin & Sons Ltd
1478	Wilkes & Curtis Ltd
1481	Wilkes & Curtis Ltd
1483	Wilkes & Curtis Ltd
1485	Wilkes & Curtis Ltd
1486	Wilkes & Curtis Ltd
1489	Wilkes & Curtis Ltd
1490	Wilkes & Curtis Ltd
1491	Wilkes & Curtis Ltd
1492	Wilkes & Curtis Ltd
1493	Ashmolean Museum, Oxford
1495	Wilkes & Curtis Ltd
1497	Wilkes & Curtis Ltd
1498	Morton & Eden Ltd
1500	Wilkes & Curtis Ltd
1501	Wilkes & Curtis Ltd
1502	Wilkes & Curtis Ltd
1504	Wilkes & Curtis Ltd
1507	Morton & Eden Ltd
1508	Wilkes & Curtis Ltd
1510	Ashmolean Museum, Oxford
1512	Wilkes & Curtis Ltd
1514	Wilkes & Curtis Ltd
1515	Wilkes & Curtis Ltd
1517	Wilkes & Curtis Ltd
1519	Wilkes & Curtis Ltd
1520	Wilkes & Curtis Ltd
1521	Wilkes & Curtis Ltd
1523	Wilkes & Curtis Ltd
1524	Wilkes & Curtis Ltd
1525	Wilkes & Curtis Ltd
1527	Wilkes & Curtis Ltd
1529	Wilkes & Curtis Ltd
1531	Wilkes & Curtis Ltd
1533	Wilkes & Curtis Ltd
1535	Wilkes & Curtis Ltd
1536	Wilkes & Curtis Ltd
1544	A. H. Baldwin & Sons Ltd
1548	Wilkes & Curtis Ltd
1551	Wilkes & Curtis Ltd
1552	Wilkes & Curtis Ltd
1554	Wilkes & Curtis Ltd
1556	Morton & Eden Ltd
1559	Morton & Eden Ltd
1561	Morton & Eden Ltd
1562	Wilkes & Curtis Ltd
1567	Ashmolean Museum, Oxford
1568	Wilkes & Curtis Ltd
1571	Wilkes & Curtis Ltd
1572	Ashmolean Museum, Oxford
1573	Wilkes & Curtis Ltd

1574	Ashmolean Museum, Oxford
1575	Ashmolean Museum, Oxford
1576	Wilkes & Curtis Ltd
1577	Ashmolean Museum, Oxford
1578	Ashmolean Museum, Oxford
1579	Ashmolean Museum, Oxford
1580	Ashmolean Museum, Oxford
1582	Wilkes & Curtis Ltd
1583	Wilkes & Curtis Ltd
1586	Wilkes & Curtis Ltd
1587	Ashmolean Museum, Oxford
1588	Ashmolean Museum, Oxford
1591	Ashmolean Museum, Oxford
1592	Wilkes & Curtis Ltd
1594	Wilkes & Curtis Ltd
1598	Ashmolean Museum, Oxford
1599	Ashmolean Museum, Oxford
1601	Ashmolean Museum, Oxford
1604	Wilkes & Curtis Ltd
1607	Ashmolean Museum, Oxford
1609	Wilkes & Curtis Ltd
1610	Ashmolean Museum, Oxford
1612	Ashmolean Museum, Oxford
1613	Ashmolean Museum, Oxford
1615	Ashmolean Museum, Oxford
1622	Wilkes & Curtis Ltd
1625	Ashmolean Museum, Oxford
1626	Wilkes & Curtis Ltd
1627	Ashmolean Museum, Oxford
1632	Wilkes & Curtis Ltd
1648	Wilkes & Curtis Ltd
1651	Wilkes & Curtis Ltd
1652	Ashmolean Museum, Oxford
1653	Wilkes & Curtis Ltd
1654	Morton & Eden Ltd
1655	Ashmolean Museum, Oxford
1656	Wilkes & Curtis Ltd
1659	Ashmolean Museum, Oxford
1661	Wilkes & Curtis Ltd
1668	Wilkes & Curtis Ltd
1669	Wilkes & Curtis Ltd
1672	Wilkes & Curtis Ltd
1673	Wilkes & Curtis Ltd
1674	Ashmolean Museum, Oxford
1675	Wilkes & Curtis Ltd
1676	Wilkes & Curtis Ltd
1677	Wilkes & Curtis Ltd
1678	Wilkes & Curtis Ltd
1681	A. H. Baldwin & Sons Ltd
1683	Ashmolean Museum, Oxford
1690	Morton & Eden Ltd
1696	Wilkes & Curtis Ltd
1697	Wilkes & Curtis Ltd
1698	Ashmolean Museum, Oxford
1700	Wilkes & Curtis Ltd

1702	Wilkes & Curtis Ltd
1703	Ashmolean Museum, Oxford
1706	Ashmolean Museum, Oxford
1707	Wilkes & Curtis Ltd
1714	Wilkes & Curtis Ltd
1716	Ashmolean Museum, Oxford
1718	Wilkes & Curtis Ltd
1720	Ashmolean Museum, Oxford
1721	Wilkes & Curtis Ltd
1724	Wilkes & Curtis Ltd
1731	Ashmolean Museum, Oxford
1743	Ashmolean Museum, Oxford
1745	Wilkes & Curtis Ltd
1746	Wilkes & Curtis Ltd
1747	Wilkes & Curtis Ltd
1749	Wilkes & Curtis Ltd
1750	Wilkes & Curtis Ltd
1753	Wilkes & Curtis Ltd
1754	Wilkes & Curtis Ltd
1757	Wilkes & Curtis Ltd
1761	Wilkes & Curtis Ltd
1762	Wilkes & Curtis Ltd
1763	Wilkes & Curtis Ltd
1768	Wilkes & Curtis Ltd
1770	Wilkes & Curtis Ltd
1774	Wilkes & Curtis Ltd
1786	Wilkes & Curtis Ltd
1789	Ashmolean Museum, Oxford
1798	Ashmolean Museum, Oxford
1801	Wilkes & Curtis Ltd
1811	Ashmolean Museum, Oxford
1814	Wilkes & Curtis Ltd
1815	Wilkes & Curtis Ltd
1816	Wilkes & Curtis Ltd
1817	Wilkes & Curtis Ltd
1818	Wilkes & Curtis Ltd
1821	Wilkes & Curtis Ltd
1823	Wilkes & Curtis Ltd
1829	A. H. Baldwin & Sons Ltd
1830	Ashmolean Museum, Oxford
1833	Ashmolean Museum, Oxford
1835	Ashmolean Museum, Oxford
1837	A. H. Baldwin & Sons Ltd
1839	Ashmolean Museum, Oxford
1847	Wilkes & Curtis Ltd
1849	Ashmolean Museum, Oxford
1851	Wilkes & Curtis Ltd
1857	A. H. Baldwin & Sons Ltd
1870	Ashmolean Museum, Oxford
1871	Ashmolean Museum, Oxford
1876	Spink & Son Ltd
1879	Wilkes & Curtis Ltd
1881	Wilkes & Curtis Ltd
1883	Wilkes & Curtis Ltd
1885	Wilkes & Curtis Ltd

1891	Classical Numismatic Group, Inc.
1899	Wilkes & Curtis Ltd
1901	Ashmolean Museum, Oxford
1902	Ashmolean Museum, Oxford
1904	Ashmolean Museum, Oxford
1914	Spink & Son Ltd
1917	Wilkes & Curtis Ltd
1918	Wilkes & Curtis Ltd
1919	Ashmolean Museum, Oxford
1921	Wilkes & Curtis Ltd
1923	Spink & Son Ltd
1926	Ashmolean Museum, Oxford
1927	Ashmolean Museum, Oxford
1933	Wilkes & Curtis Ltd
1936	Ashmolean Museum, Oxford
1939	Ashmolean Museum, Oxford
1940	Classical Numismatic Group, Inc.
1941	Wilkes & Curtis Ltd
1946	Classical Numismatic Group, Inc.
1947	Morton & Eden Ltd
1948	Ashmolean Museum, Oxford
1950	Ashmolean Museum, Oxford
1955	Ashmolean Museum, Oxford
1965	Wilkes & Curtis Ltd
1971	Wilkes & Curtis Ltd
1974	Wilkes & Curtis Ltd
1976	Wilkes & Curtis Ltd
1979	Wilkes & Curtis Ltd
1987	Wilkes & Curtis Ltd
1991	Spink & Son Ltd
1995	Wilkes & Curtis Ltd
1996	Wilkes & Curtis Ltd
1997	Wilkes & Curtis Ltd
1998	Wilkes & Curtis Ltd
2001	Wilkes & Curtis Ltd
2004	Wilkes & Curtis Ltd
2012	Ashmolean Museum, Oxford
2021	Wilkes & Curtis Ltd
2023	Wilkes & Curtis Ltd
2025	Ashmolean Museum, Oxford
2027	Ashmolean Museum, Oxford
2029	Ashmolean Museum, Oxford
2031	Ashmolean Museum, Oxford
2033	Ashmolean Museum, Oxford
2034	Ashmolean Museum, Oxford
2035	Ashmolean Museum, Oxford
2036	Ashmolean Museum, Oxford
2038	Wilkes & Curtis Ltd
2040	Wilkes & Curtis Ltd
2042	Ashmolean Museum, Oxford
2043	Ashmolean Museum, Oxford
2044	Ashmolean Museum, Oxford
2046	Wilkes & Curtis Ltd
2048	Ashmolean Museum, Oxford
2051	Ashmolean Museum, Oxford
2055	Ashmolean Museum, Oxford
2065	Ashmolean Museum, Oxford
2066	Ashmolean Museum, Oxford
2068	A. H. Baldwin & Sons Ltd
2069	Morton & Eden Ltd
2074	Ashmolean Museum, Oxford
2075	Ashmolean Museum, Oxford
2079	Ashmolean Museum, Oxford
2080	Ashmolean Museum, Oxford
2082	Wilkes & Curtis Ltd
2086	Wilkes & Curtis Ltd
2087	Ashmolean Museum, Oxford
2091	Ashmolean Museum, Oxford
2096	Spink & Son Ltd
2097	Wilkes & Curtis Ltd
2098	Ashmolean Museum, Oxford
2099	Ashmolean Museum, Oxford
2106	Ashmolean Museum, Oxford
2107	Ashmolean Museum, Oxford
2109	A. H. Baldwin & Sons Ltd
2110	Wilkes & Curtis Ltd
2111	Ashmolean Museum, Oxford
2114	Wilkes & Curtis Ltd
2115	Wilkes & Curtis Ltd
2116	Ashmolean Museum, Oxford
2126	Wilkes & Curtis Ltd
2128	Wilkes & Curtis Ltd
2129	Wilkes & Curtis Ltd
2130	A. H. Baldwin & Sons Ltd
2131	Ashmolean Museum, Oxford
2132	Ashmolean Museum, Oxford
2133	Wilkes & Curtis Ltd
2135	Ashmolean Museum, Oxford
2138	Wilkes & Curtis Ltd
2139	A. H. Baldwin & Sons Ltd
2140	Wilkes & Curtis Ltd
2141	Ashmolean Museum, Oxford
2143	Wilkes & Curtis Ltd
2145	Ashmolean Museum, Oxford
2148	Wilkes & Curtis Ltd
2149	Ashmolean Museum, Oxford
2152	Morton & Eden Ltd
2153	Ashmolean Museum, Oxford
2154	Morton & Eden Ltd
2155	Wilkes & Curtis Ltd
2159	Wilkes & Curtis Ltd
2160	Wilkes & Curtis Ltd
2161	Ashmolean Museum, Oxford
2165	Wilkes & Curtis Ltd
2166	Wilkes & Curtis Ltd
2169	A. H. Baldwin & Sons Ltd
2170	Ashmolean Museum, Oxford
2172	Morton & Eden Ltd
2173	Wilkes & Curtis Ltd
2174	Wilkes & Curtis Ltd

2175	Ashmolean Museum, Oxford
2183	Ashmolean Museum, Oxford
2187	Wilkes & Curtis Ltd
2192	A. H. Baldwin & Sons Ltd
2193	Wilkes & Curtis Ltd
2194	Wilkes & Curtis Ltd
2208	A. H. Baldwin & Sons Ltd
2210	Wilkes & Curtis Ltd
2213	Ashmolean Museum, Oxford
2214	Ashmolean Museum, Oxford
2217	Wilkes & Curtis Ltd
2219	Wilkes & Curtis Ltd
2221	Wilkes & Curtis Ltd
2222	Ashmolean Museum, Oxford
2223	Wilkes & Curtis Ltd
2226	Morton & Eden Ltd
2228	Wilkes & Curtis Ltd
2230	Morton & Eden Ltd
2232	Ashmolean Museum, Oxford
2234	Wilkes & Curtis Ltd
2239	Wilkes & Curtis Ltd
2240	Ashmolean Museum, Oxford
2241	Wilkes & Curtis Ltd
2248	Wilkes & Curtis Ltd
2251	Wilkes & Curtis Ltd
2257	Wilkes & Curtis Ltd
2264	Wilkes & Curtis Ltd
2266	Wilkes & Curtis Ltd
2267	Wilkes & Curtis Ltd
2271	Wilkes & Curtis Ltd
2272	Wilkes & Curtis Ltd
2278	A. H. Baldwin & Sons Ltd
2282	Ashmolean Museum, Oxford
2284	Spink & Son Ltd
2291	Wilkes & Curtis Ltd
2292	Wilkes & Curtis Ltd
2296	Wilkes & Curtis Ltd
2298	Ashmolean Museum, Oxford
2300	Wilkes & Curtis Ltd
2301	Ashmolean Museum, Oxford
2310	Ashmolean Museum, Oxford
2311	Wilkes & Curtis Ltd
2312	Wilkes & Curtis Ltd
2314	Ashmolean Museum, Oxford
2316	Wilkes & Curtis Ltd
2317	Wilkes & Curtis Ltd
2319	Ashmolean Museum, Oxford
2321	Wilkes & Curtis Ltd
2323	Wilkes & Curtis Ltd
2325	Ashmolean Museum, Oxford
2328	Wilkes & Curtis Ltd
2329	Wilkes & Curtis Ltd
2330	Wilkes & Curtis Ltd
2331	Wilkes & Curtis Ltd
2334	Ashmolean Museum, Oxford
2335	Wilkes & Curtis Ltd
2336	Wilkes & Curtis Ltd
2341	Wilkes & Curtis Ltd
2342	Wilkes & Curtis Ltd
2346	Wilkes & Curtis Ltd
2347	Wilkes & Curtis Ltd
2351	Wilkes & Curtis Ltd
2353	Wilkes & Curtis Ltd
2361	Ashmolean Museum, Oxford
2363	Ashmolean Museum, Oxford
2364	Wilkes & Curtis Ltd
2365	Ashmolean Museum, Oxford
2366	Spink & Son Ltd
2369	Ashmolean Museum, Oxford
2370	Ashmolean Museum, Oxford
2371	Ashmolean Museum, Oxford
2378	A. H. Baldwin & Sons Ltd
2380	Wilkes & Curtis Ltd
2381	Wilkes & Curtis Ltd
2384	Wilkes & Curtis Ltd
2386	Ashmolean Museum, Oxford
2389	Wilkes & Curtis Ltd
2390	Wilkes & Curtis Ltd
2391	Wilkes & Curtis Ltd
2395	Ashmolean Museum, Oxford
2398	Ashmolean Museum, Oxford
2401	Wilkes & Curtis Ltd
2412	Wilkes & Curtis Ltd
2430	Wilkes & Curtis Ltd
2433	A. H. Baldwin & Sons Ltd
2435	Wilkes & Curtis Ltd
2438	A. H. Baldwin & Sons Ltd
2441	Wilkes & Curtis Ltd
2443	Wilkes & Curtis Ltd
2447	A. H. Baldwin & Sons Ltd
2448	Wilkes & Curtis Ltd
2454	Wilkes & Curtis Ltd
2460	Morton & Eden Ltd
2466	A. H. Baldwin & Sons Ltd
2470	Wilkes & Curtis Ltd
2471	Wilkes & Curtis Ltd
2479	Spink & Son Ltd
2480	Wilkes & Curtis Ltd
2481	Private collection, UK
2483	Private collection, UK
2488	A. H. Baldwin & Sons Ltd
2490	Wilkes & Curtis Ltd
2494	Wilkes & Curtis Ltd
2495	Wilkes & Curtis Ltd
2496	Wilkes & Curtis Ltd
2497	Wilkes & Curtis Ltd
2500	Spink & Son Ltd
2501	Wilkes & Curtis Ltd
2505	Wilkes & Curtis Ltd
2507	Wilkes & Curtis Ltd

2517	A. H. Baldwin & Sons Ltd
2518	Wilkes & Curtis Ltd
2520	Wilkes & Curtis Ltd
2524	A. H. Baldwin & Sons Ltd
2525	Wilkes & Curtis Ltd
2529	A. H. Baldwin & Sons Ltd
2534	A. H. Baldwin & Sons Ltd
2544	A. H. Baldwin & Sons Ltd
2592	Wilkes & Curtis Ltd
2599	Wilkes & Curtis Ltd
2615	Wilkes & Curtis Ltd
2616	Wilkes & Curtis Ltd
2622	Wilkes & Curtis Ltd
2625	Wilkes & Curtis Ltd
2626	Wilkes & Curtis Ltd
2629	Wilkes & Curtis Ltd
2632	Wilkes & Curtis Ltd
2634	Wilkes & Curtis Ltd
2635	Wilkes & Curtis Ltd
2636	A. H. Baldwin & Sons Ltd
2637	Wilkes & Curtis Ltd
2639	A. H. Baldwin & Sons Ltd
2640	Wilkes & Curtis Ltd
2645	Wilkes & Curtis Ltd
2648	Wilkes & Curtis Ltd
2650	Wilkes & Curtis Ltd
2655	Spink & Son Ltd
2657	Spink & Son Ltd
2660	A. H. Baldwin & Sons Ltd
2661	Wilkes & Curtis Ltd
2666	Spink & Son Ltd
2668	A. H. Baldwin & Sons Ltd
2669	Wilkes & Curtis Ltd
2670	Spink & Son Ltd
2671	Wilkes & Curtis Ltd
2674	Spink & Son Ltd
2679	Classical Numismatic Group, Inc.
2681	A. H. Baldwin & Sons Ltd
2684	Wilkes & Curtis Ltd
2685	Wilkes & Curtis Ltd
2688	Wilkes & Curtis Ltd
2708	A. H. Baldwin & Sons Ltd
2712	A. H. Baldwin & Sons Ltd
2713	Wilkes & Curtis Ltd
2716	Spink & Son Ltd
2719	A. H. Baldwin & Sons Ltd
2720	Wilkes & Curtis Ltd
2727	Wilkes & Curtis Ltd
2729	A. H. Baldwin & Sons Ltd
2733	Wilkes & Curtis Ltd
2734	Wilkes & Curtis Ltd
2751	Wilkes & Curtis Ltd
2774	A. H. Baldwin & Sons Ltd
2779	A. H. Baldwin & Sons Ltd
2789	A. H. Baldwin & Sons Ltd
2814	A. H. Baldwin & Sons Ltd
2816	Wilkes & Curtis Ltd
2823	A. H. Baldwin & Sons Ltd
2837	A. H. Baldwin & Sons Ltd
2847	Spink & Son Ltd
2856	A. H. Baldwin & Sons Ltd
2858	Wilkes & Curtis Ltd
2863	Spink & Son Ltd
2864	Wilkes & Curtis Ltd
2872	Wilkes & Curtis Ltd
2874	Wilkes & Curtis Ltd
2879	A. H. Baldwin & Sons Ltd
2881	Private collection, UK
2883	Private collection, UK
2890	A. H. Baldwin & Sons Ltd
2897	Wilkes & Curtis Ltd
2899	Private collection, UK
2907	Classical Numismatic Group, Inc.
2908	Private collection, UK
2909	Private collection, UK
2910	Private collection, UK
2911	Private collection, UK
2915	A. H. Baldwin & Sons Ltd
2916	Wilkes & Curtis Ltd
2917	Private collection, UK
2919	Wilkes & Curtis Ltd
2938	Wilkes & Curtis Ltd
2941	Wilkes & Curtis Ltd
2947	Private collection, UK
2959	Private collection, UK
2974	Wilkes & Curtis Ltd
2977	Spink & Son Ltd
2982	Private collection, UK
2987	Jean Elsen & ses Fils s.a.
2989	Jean Elsen & ses Fils s.a.
2990	Wilkes & Curtis Ltd
2991	Jean Elsen & ses Fils s.a.
2993	Jean Elsen & ses Fils s.a.
2995	Jean Elsen & ses Fils s.a.
2997	Jean Elsen & ses Fils s.a.

INDEX

Abbadid	55
Abbasid	33
Abbasid Copper	47
Abbasid Governors of Tabaristan	14
Afrasiyabid	220
Afrighid	157
Afshinid	156
Aftasid of Badajoz	58
Aghlabid	62
Alanya, Beylik of	139
Algarve	59
'Alid	170
al-Khuttal, Amirs of	149
Almohad	67
Almoravid	66
'Amirid of Valencia	55
Andaraba, Amirs of	158
'Annazid	170
Anti-Aghlabid Revolt	64
Anti-Hamdanid Revolt	83
Aq Qoyunlu	230
Arab-Armenian	13
Arab-Bukharan	14
Arab-Byzantine	18
Arab-Hephthalite	14
Arab-Khwarezm	13
Arab-Sasanian	1
Artuqid of Hisn Kayfa & Amid	111
Artuqid of Khartabirt	115
Artuqid of Mardin	116
Assassins of Alamut (see Batinid)	
'Athar, Amirs of	101
Aydin, Beylik of	139
Ayyubid	86
Ayyubid of Aleppo	89
Ayyubid of al-Jazira	91
Ayyubid of Damascus	90
Ayyubid of Hamah	90
Ayyubid of Hisn Kayfa	91
Ayyubid of the Yemen	105
Badakhshan, Shahs of	200
Bahmanid	253
Balkh, Amir of	191
Banijurid	148
Banu Hilal	65
Banu Mismar	100
Barghawatid of Sfax	66
Batinid	189
Bavandid	173
Begteginid	130
Begtimurid	130
Bengal, Sultans of	245
Bukhti Kurds	219
Burid	85
Bust, Amirs of	157
Buwayhid	161
Chaghatayid	197
Chupanid	216
Cordoba, Kings of	58
Countermarked Byzantine Coins	132
Crete, Amirs of	75
Danishmendid	131
Dehli, Sultans of	235
Denia, Slave Kingdom of	56
Dhu'l-Nunid of Toledo	57
Dulafid	143
Eastern Sistan	11
Eretnid	140
Fars, Atabegs of	189
Fatimid	77
Fatimid Partisans	101
Firuzanid	173
Germiyan, Beylik of	139
Ghaznavid	175
Ghorid	192
Ghorid of Bamiyan	193
Golden Horde	200
Great Mongol	195
Great Seljuq	183
Gujarat, Sultans of	258
Habbarid of Sind	234
Hadhabani Kurds	174
Hafsid	69
Hamdanid	82
Hamidid	139
Hammudid of Malaga	54
Hammudid of Wadi Lau	55
Harthamid	144
Hasanwayhid	169
Hazaraspid	217
Hudid of Denia	56
Hudid of Murcia	59
Hudid of Tudela	57
Hudid of Zaragoza	56
Husaynid	220

284

Husaynid Sharifs	107
Idrisid	61
Idrisid Contemporaries	62
Ikhshidid	76
Ildegizid	187
Ildegizid Vassals	188
Ilkhanid	204
'Imranid	174
Injuyid	217
Isfendiyarid	140
Jalayrid	218
Jastanid	169
Jaunpur, Sultans of	257
Julandid	169
Kakwayhid	170
Kalpi, Sultans of	258
Karamanid	139
Karesi, Beylik of	138
Kart	221
Kashmir, Sultans of	264
Khaqanid	188
Kharijites	62
Khawlanid	103
Khazars	157
Khazrunid	65
Khujistanid	144
Khwarizmshahs	190
Kilwa, Sultans of	110
Kurds of Adharbayjan	160
Kurzuwan, Malik of	197
Lorca, Amirs of	59
Lu'lu'id	125
Madura, Sultans of	253
Mahdid of Zabid	104
Mallorca, Kings of	56
Malwa, Sultans of	261
Mamluk	91
Marwanid	84
Mehrabanid	223
Menkujakid	131
Menteshe, Beylik of	138
Merinid	72
Mertola & Silves, Kings of	58
Midrarid	65
Mirdasid	84
Mogadishu, Sultans of	110
Muhtajid	157
Mukramid	109
Multan, Amirs of	234
Murabitid (see Almoravid)	
Murcia, Kings of	58
Musha'sha'	232
Muwahhid (see Almohad)	
Muzaffarid	217

Najjahid	103
Nasrid	59
Nishapur, Amirs of	187
Numayrid	85
Oman, Amirs of	109
Oman, Governors of	108
Pishkinid	189
Proto-Qarakhanid	178
Qadis of Sivas	141
Qalhati Amirs of Hormuz	216
Qarakhanid	178
Qarakhanid Vassals	183
Qara Qoyunlu	229
Qarlughid	194
Qarmatid	77
Qunduz, Amir of	233
Qutlughkhanid	215
Rassid (1st period)	100
Rassid (2nd period)	104
Rassid (3rd period)	108
Rasulid	106
Rawwadid	174
Revolutionary Period	31
Riyahid	67
Saffarid	144
Sajid	159
Salduqid	130
Salghurid	190
Sallarid	168
Samanid	149
Samanid of Akhsikath	156
Samudra-Pasai	267
Saqchi, Khanate of	204
Sarbadarid	220
Saruhan, Beylik of	138
Seljuq of Hamadan	186
Seljuq of Kirman	187
Seljuq of Rum	133
Seljuq of Syria	85
Seljuq of Western Iran	186
Shabankara, Atabegs of	216
Shaddadid	160
Sharaf Khans	220
Shirvanshahs	229
Sicily	86
Sind, Sultans of	234
Sufid	223
Sulamid	188
Sulayhid	103
Sulaymanid	64
Su'lukid	160
Sumaydihid of Almeria	57
Sutayid	219
Taghaytimurid	221

Tahirid (Iran)	142
Tahirid (Yemen)	108
Taifas Almoravides	58
Tarafid	102
Timurid	224
Tortosa, Kingdom of	57
Tulunid	74
Umayyad Copper	29
Umayyad Gold	22
Umayyad Silver	25
Umayyad of Spain	50
'Uqaylid	83
Volga Bulgars	157
Wajihid	108
Wakhsh, Amirs of	191
Walid	221
Warwarliz, Amirs of	159
Wattasid	73
Yazd, Atabegs of	216
Yun, Amirs of	174
Zanj Rebellion	143
Zanzibar, Sultans of	110
Zaydi Imams of Hawsam	168
Zengid of al-Jazira	129
Zengid of Mosul	122
Zengid of Shahrazur	129
Zengid of Sinjar	127
Zengid of Syria	126
Zirid	65
Zirid of Granada	55
Ziyadid	102
Ziyanid	71
Ziyarid	171
Ziyarid of the Jibal	173
Zuray'id	104